Introduction To Evolutionary Astrology

Written by Tashi Powers
Evolutionary Astrologer

Published by Dakini Books 2020

©2020 Tashi Powers
FIRST EDITION

July 2020
Cover art by:Varvara
Book Design by: Varvara
ISBN: **978-1-7379180-1-1**

Independently Published
California, USA

For information on this and other works visit:

@Tashiastrodakini

www.facebook.com/Astrodakini

www.enlighteningtimes.com

This book is dedicated to:

All the dearest souls on this planet who share a connection with Natural Law.

The Ninth Wave of Unity Consciousness that is helping Humanity and Gaia ascend.

Evolutionary Astrologers, learning to communicate with the Planets, Stars, Galactic Equator Alignments, the Galactic Center.

The Evolutionary Astrological paradigm, transmitted to Jeffrey Wolf Green by Sri Yukteswar, from which I derive much inspiration.

Yogis and Meditators aspiring to open your third eye to the wonders of the inner dimensions.

Daemon Souls who are learning to use Mother Nature's Building Blocks.

Anyone searching for how Devas help Humanity .

The Toolbox of Co-creation.

TESTIMONIALS

Personal experience tells me that Tashi Powers is the real deal—and the Basics of Evolutionary Astrology is a superb guide that will inform and enlighten in ways that most other astrology books simply cannot. It is the work of a true master of her craft, rich food for the inquiring mind. —Whitley Strieber

Truly insightful, deep and a great tool for managing life. Have listened to the recording twice over and gained sustained learnings beyond just the face to face session. Powerful stuff. —RS

My first session with Tashi felt like the first time I was truly seen. She is plugged into a Divine Channel that echoes truth and crystalline insight . —Serena Ryder

Tashi is more than just an astrologer! She is an exceptional healer and psychotherapist. She knew I was a holistic MD from just my chart. She knew I was under immense stress which she has helped me with.— Anonymous

I have seen dozens of astrologers and there is no one like Tashi Powers. The scale of a reading with Tashi is multi-dimensional. Tashi can zero in on a minute interpersonal dynamic and then zoom out to Big Picture purpose. I've never felt like I have been seen so holistically before.   With that said, the insights I received were also extremely practical and actionable.—LR

My reading with Tashi was one of the most profound experiences of my life. It felt as if she knew me better than I know myself. The advice she gave me was SO spot on and so aligned with what I have always known deep down. And the advice was rather a guidance in a positive direction—subtle, forward moving, and showing me towards my life's purpose/destiny. She is extremely knowledgeable and wise and I am truly impressed by her ability. I am in awe of this woman. —Josefina

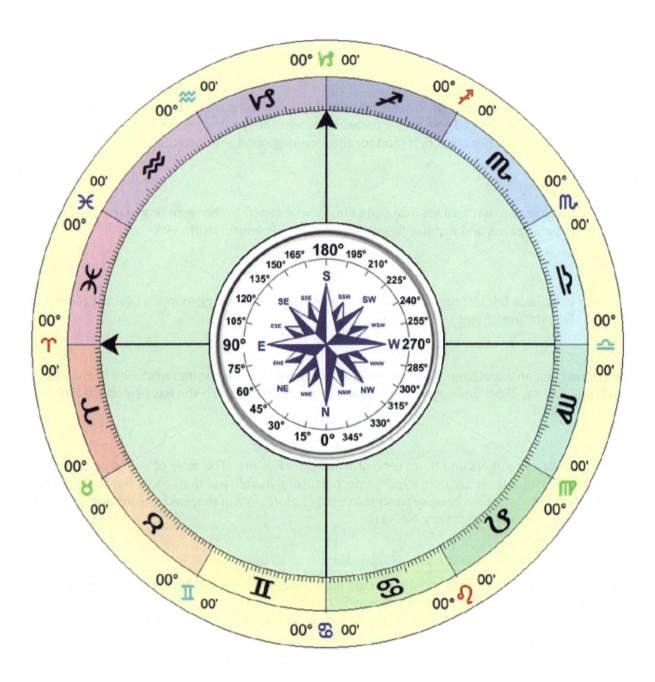

TABLE OF CONTENTS

INTRODUCTION

by Kevin Stein

You are about to experience one of the great adventures in life, even perhaps the ultimate one. By opening this book, you have made a choice to take an amazing journey through the heavens to discover what makes you a truly unique and active participant in the universe.

You will learn about the cycles and patterns that have been studied for thousands of years by various cultures once driven by the desire to make connections between what happens above and below the stars, planets, moon, and our home world. More important, you will find out how to practically apply the principles that have been drawn over time to make your own outer and inner life more productive, successful, loving, and expansive in ways you only dreamed of.

Ancient cultures did not throw out knowledge and systems that work. It's been the same with tribal cultures—when survival is key, the unproven is an unnecessary weight on day-to-day life and worldly progress. The impulse to make sense of the stars led our species to look above and beyond to gather the stars and group them together as constellations to tell their stories through myth and legend. It is said the stars once spoke to us, but that we forgot their language.

Tashi Powers has created a wonderful introduction to Evolutionary Astrology that is the culmination of decades of deep experience with the human condition and life cycle in all its phases. Drawing from both Eastern and Western world traditions of star wisdom including Vedic and Evolutionary Astrology, she has also been inspired to inform her original approach with treasures from feng shui, geomancy, the ley line system, healing gems, crystals, and mantra—all presented in a beautifully relatable, visual format. These seemingly different streams are drawn together through her magical lens into a rich confluence and spiritual offering of singular vision.

True to her humble form, Tashi is the first to recognize that her book is not all her own doing but a stellar gift informed by a gathering of angels and other forces of light. What she has done with this new book and future publications is to pull back the veil in a highly practical way on the pulse of time, and the mysteries of destiny, fate, and free will. Her divine contribution will empower dedicated souls to once again know that they, too, can learn once again with joy how to speak the language of the stars.

ACKNOWLEDGMENTS

It takes a village...and this was mine to accomplish the writing of this book:

My two guardian angels, who told me a few years ago that I would have to find solitude and write. Over time, I have come to recognize that any attempt I might make to do otherwise would be met with their admonishment and not so gentle reminders to settle in and get down to business. They made it clear that I needed to leave a legacy about how to navigate the Cosmos, planets, and the archetypal star frequencies which make up the signs, houses, and the natal horoscope.

My EA Astrology teacher, Jeffrey Wolf Green's inspiration and quotes permeate this book as it does the soul of all his students. I remain eternally grateful to JWG and his generous heart and soul. The same spirit goes out to the EA community of Astrologers, who practice sharing, caring, and inclusion.

My dear friend and artist, Leigh J. McCloskey, who so generously shared his Tarot images and insights, taken from his Masterpiece: Tarot ReVISIONed Original Artwork & Text. For more information on this and his other wonderful works, please visit: www.leighjmccloskey.com

My graphic artist, Varvara, whose patient midwifery has helped birth this book.

I can name a few other teachers who have been consequential to my studies. These include Marion March. I thank her for gifting me with expertise in Electional Astrology. Heartfelt gratitude to Judy Johns, who taught me Political Astrology, and how to use the Solstice and Equinox blueprint charts.

Joseph Campbell, who instructed me as a nineteen-year-old student to "Follow my bliss." Jack Schwartz. who taught me to see auras. Kalu Rinpoche, my root Lama, who taught me to morph into source. Trungpa Rinpoche, who got me to study the dharma. I am practicing the Kundalini yoga tradition currently.

My current team, including Kevin Stein, who line edited the book with a deep understanding of both Astrology and marketing which hopefully makes the book more accessible to all seekers.

My friends, who haven't seen much of me, thank you for being there, you know who you are.
My daughter, who always has my back. And is the light of my soul.
My students, for whom I burn the midnight oil.

THE BASICS OF EVOLUTIONARY ASTROLOGY
by the Author

THE 12 LETTER ALPHABET IS ABOVE. Each zodiacal sign corresponds with a house number, next is the glyph of the sign, the associated animal and the sign's ruling Planet.

Evolutionary Astrology—EA—as we call it, teaches you Natural Law. Jeffrey Wolf Green describes Natural Law as"... *the Laws set in motion by the Source Of All Thing, one of those laws relative to human beings, is to give, share, and include. Thus, when humans live in accordance with Natural Laws all will give according to their capacity, and the natural roles each human has in the context of the social whole that they are part of. Sadly, this Natural Law has been perverted and turned upside down. That Natural Law has now become one of self-interest and exclusion which is not a Natural Law at all. As a Soul progressively de-conditions from all the man-made and artificial conditioning that has been manifesting since around 7,000 BCE forwards the Natural Law, and desire, to give, share and include begins to resurface into the consciousness of the Soul.*"

EA is also an exploration of the steps a soul is taking, through successive lifetimes, to further its grasp of Natural Law, as they progressively understand the order in the Cosmos. It shows the Planetary system around us, and how our Galaxy works. It shows us the timing of events. It teaches us about our position on our karmic journey and what are the karmic necessities we will face. It shows us how to reach for the greater good. It warns us how Planetary and Cosmic frequencies appear in our lives when distorted or avoided. It gives us stepping stones to integrate the many facets of this life, as we overcome challenges, and learn to thrive.

Your birth chart delineates this life's journey. The Chart is a wheel of 12 houses. On the left side of the page is the sign of the zodiac that is rising over earth's horizon at the time of your birth.
You will need an accurate birth time to construct the astrological natal chart. You will also need the day, month, year and place of birth. Computers will then calculate the chart. This can be done for yourself, your family, children, friends, as well as for events.

In this book you will be given keywords for the 12 Signs, Planets, and Houses. You can learn how to read a chart once you can synthesize different aspects of this 12 letter alphabet in your chart. The Planets are inside the 12 houses and need to be read by both House and Zodiac Sign.

Planets rise in the East. The Sign on the 1h cusp is your Ascendant or Rising Sign. It is the degree of the Zodiac that was rising on the Celestial Equator. Then moving East to West the Planets and the Moon will reach their zenith at high noon in the South, called the Midheaven. Continuing along the Ecliptic Planets then set in the West around Sunset, and this point of the chart is the 7h cusp, called the Descendant. The last trip of the 24 hour days for the Planets as they round the chart is from West to North. The Planets hit the Midnight point, called the I.C., then start to rise moving back towards the horizon, or the Ascendant.

How To Use This Book

We designed this book to warmly welcome you to the expansive, venerable path of Evolutionary Astrology. Learning this new language of theStars should be easy and fun, so we encourage you to go at your own pace. There is no "right" way to read this book. Many readers will flip the pages and go directly to discover what their own Sun sign means or may skip to other sections that most interest them—to the signs ruling family and friends, for example. Others will travel at a more linear pace, starting at the beginning of the text. Either way, we encourage you to read all of the chapters in sequence, eventually to understand their evolutionary progression.

Astrology is an ancient study of patterns and cycles and how they affect human behavior. By reading the signs in order, you will see how they reflect a natural order that is foundational to developing a holistic understanding of how they all work together. To get a quick take on the relationship of the planets and signs to their respective rulers, the chart below will be helpful. For those readers who are interested in taking a deeper dive into more advanced Evolutionary Astrological concepts, the sections on the Daemon Soul and Pluto Paradigm will be of special interest, located at the back of the book.

Above all, the Planetary energies, Sun signs, and houses describe a cosmic evolutionary course that is perfect and divine. Your study of the starry wisdom will yield countless rewards as you apply them to your own purpose. As above, so below.

HOUSE	SIGN	PLANETARY RULER		HOUSE	SIGN	PLANETARY RULER
1	ARIES—♈	MARS		7	LIBRA—♎	VENUS
2	TAURUS—♉	VENUS		8	SCORPIO—♏	PLUTO
3	GEMINI—♊	MERCURY		9	SAGITTARIUS—	JUPITER
4	CANCER—♋	MOON		10	CAPRICORN—♑	SATURN
5	LEO—♌	SUN		11	AQUARIUS—♒	URANUS
6	VIRGO—♍	CHIRON/MERCURY		12	PISCES—♓	NEPTUNE

ARIES

March 21 – April 20: Tropical Western Zodiac

April 18 – May 13: Constellation of Aries

April 15 – May 15: Sidereal Zodiac

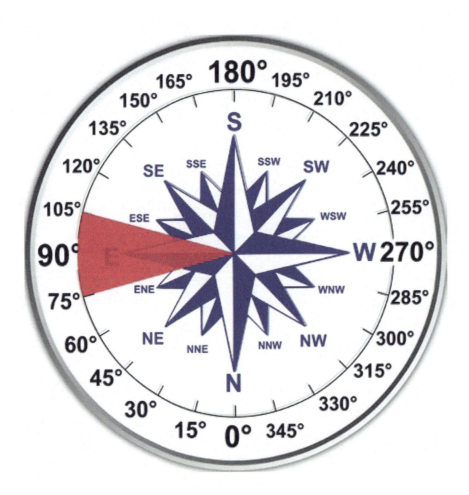

©Leigh J McCloskey,
Tarot ReVisioned

SHIVA

YANTRA

The Emperor is the 4th Key in the Tarot
Arcana and is represented astrologically
by the cardinal fire sign Aries.

THE BASICS

Aries s a member of the fire triad:

Aries	**1 house**
Leo	**5 house**
Sagittarius	**9 house**

Aries is a member of the Cardinal /Angular Houses:

Aries	**1 house**
Cancer	**4 house**
Libra	**7 house**
Capricorn	**10 house**

Mars is the Planetary ruler of the sign Aries and rules the first house, the natural house of Aries and the direction of due East.

When expressed through a higher frequency of manifestation is adventurous, dynamic, courageous, lives in the moment and is highly instinctual.

When expressed through a lower frequency of manifestation is domineering, self-absorbed, acts without consideration for others, can be violent, lacks follow through, and is intolerant.

Glyph of the Ram's Horns

Aries is a cardinal sign - dynamic.

Aries is the fire element - active.

Anatomy of Aries: Brain, Face, Teeth, Smile

Tenants of the first house take on the characteristics of Aries.

"At any point, you can cast yourself as the hero of your own story.
You get to make that choice."
—Bridget Phetasy

Planets in Houses

The First House is the on the left side of the horoscope and it correlates to Sunrise.

It relates to the exact degree and sign on the Eastern Horizon at the time of birth.

As the Earth rotates around the Sun, one degree of celestial zodiac rises above the Eastern Horizon of the Earth approximately every four minutes.

PLANETS in the FIRST HOUSE or in the sign of ARIES

⊙ **SUN** This planetary pairing strengthens the self-honoring principle as is combines self-love with self-actualization, so you become what you love.

☽ **MOON** Emotional self-reliance is strengthened by self-honoring and pioneering is possible as the emotional magic of the Moon has an ally to help her actualize her evolutionary intentions.

☿ **MERCURY** Fueling our intention to learn and name this fiery air combination gives us quick thinking, planning. Nervousness is a sign that you don't know how to slow down. It's always important with the 1st house, Mars and the Eastern position to be self-honoring.

♀ **VENUS** Social grace and innocence align well with positive vibes of Aries. Magnetism and applying our Survival skills assists us to apply healthy self-esteem to relationships.

♂ **MARS** Innocent love of life spills into this placement along with a need to slow down and see the way to be considerate of others, while exploring the best way to be self-honoring.

♃ **JUPITER** wants to expand. Don't go too fast or this double fiery optimism may get in the way of progress. Use your excitement to observe and correlate Natural Law to make the most of this placement.

♄ **SATURN** slows it all down, teaching patience so that the boundaries between self and others will be healthier.

♅ **URANUS** combined with 1, Aries or Mars will bring excitability and nervousness. Channel this energy to avoid accidents from knee jerk reaction stances.

♆ **NEPTUNE** in the 1h makes for a dreamy disposition and it will be important to choose daily endeavors that allow you to use your imaginative will forces.

♇ **PLUTO** in the 1h drives us to pursue our evolutionary path with determination and innocence. Your pioneering instincts will set you above the fray. Choose

Mars in the Houses

Mars in the First House

The East is Sunrise and Mars in this area can bring a bright, fiery energetic to your personality. Pioneering and going forward have to do with harnessing self-effort and self-initiation to harness the life force and make it matter.

Mars in the Second House

The fixed quality of Taurus allows for Mars to be deeply instinctual so that it can establish its own value system. Mars here learns the way to be authentic through the sensuality of Taurus, lending a romantic and artistic ability. This placement creates a very strong sex drive. The polarity 8h Scorpio correlates to the study of sacred sexuality and White Tantric practices.

Mars in the Third House

The search for meaning is prominent with this placement. Desire is focused on learning. Mars here can create a combative or highly independent type of communicator. Education and study can also be focused on athletic endeavors.

Mars in the Fourth House

All interactions with the 4th house lead us to search for a safe, secure and stable home life. We ultimately learn security comes from our inner strength. In this position, Mars is learning emotional self-knowledge. Once inner emotional security is established, Mars learns to be emotionally supportive of others. Doctors often have this position.

Mars in the Fifth House

Mars finds the strength to harness its evolutionary intentions through a dynamic of promoting and expressing itself creatively, in order to discover its core desire. Here Mars operates from an instinctive desire to express unique talents while reaching creative goals. Reckless risk-taking should be avoided.

Mars in the Sixth House

We place Mars here to purify our motivations, intentions, and desires. The combined energy of Virgo accelerates Mars to penetrate illusions, martyrdom, and victimhood. Once Mars in the 6th finds a spiritual practice connected to the principles of Natural Law, the habit of practice can uplift from victim/martyr scenarios. A crisis is also a 6th-house phenomenon to bring about a reality check.

Mars in the Seventh House

Wishes to challenge the status quo by initiating a diversity of relationships with others that balance the Aries need for independence vs. The 7th/Libra need for relationship. Learning to listen is tantamount to evolutionary progression. Not feeling heard, and speaking one's truth is often a challenge of this position.

Mars in the Eighth House

Penetrates the mystery of life, while learning to co-create with the *"Uni-Verse"*. Purifying the right use of power and sexuality is the goal of Mars in this house. Confronting compulsion or manipulation is the means to transformation. Deep soulful love and marriage is the reward.

Mars in the Ninth House

Brings forth a desire to know Natural Law and to discover the relativity of truth. Some ways of doing this are travel, adventure, philosophical or legal study, humor, and direct experience of Mother Nature.

Mars in the Tenth House

The Soul wishes to overcome repression created by societal constraints, oppression brought about by domination/submission, and the suppression of natural sexual desire. Ambition and success correlate to this house, and Mars here assists us in achieving our worldly desires while aligning with truth and beauty.

Mars in the Eleventh House

Is the placement of the born rebel who wishes to define her individuality. There is the potential to pioneer new ways of living, original thinking, performing, and collaborating. Detachment and experimentation are key to development. Equality consciousness must also be practiced.

Mars in the Twelfth House

Desires to penetrate the mysteries of the subconscious and make the invisible visible, giving rise to a gifted, wild imagination. Escapism and addictive delusion need to be reeled in.

"Insist on yourself, never imitate."
—*Emerson*

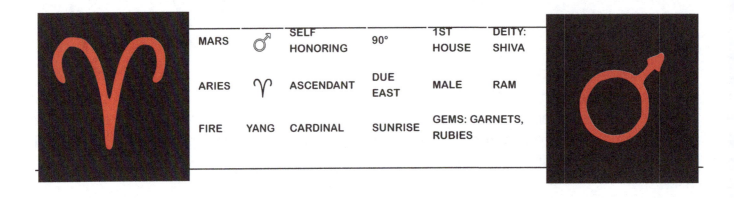

MARS	♂	SELF HONORING	90°	1ST HOUSE	DEITY: SHIVA
ARIES	♈	ASCENDANT	DUE EAST	MALE	RAM
FIRE	YANG	CARDINAL	SUNRISE	GEMS: GARNETS, RUBIES	

ARIES KEY CONCEPTS

- Pioneer and discover your love for life

- Learn to be self-honoring while balancing the need to be considerate of others

- Enhance your energy to attract adventures

- Amplify the male energy of Mars

- Strike out on your own

- Stay in the "Be Here Now" perpetual square one

- Trust your instincts

RIGHT ACTION FOR ARIES

DESIRES It is necessary to reflect upon what you desire. Reflect on the highest and best outcome for your life. Don't be self-indulgent or selfish.

ANGER Harness your projections and instead open up the paths to personal freedom.

ACTIONS May need to be directed. Decide your priorities and act on those impulses which fulfill your soul's desires.

CONSIDERATION It is necessary to take time for yourself so that you can be fully present with others. Aries is the polarity of Libra and the self/other paradigm needs full attention.

PIONEERING In Aries, we must trust our instincts and develop inner knowing.

IDENTITY The "self" is related to the archetype of Aries, so selfishness, self-centeredness, and a healthy sense of self are all some of the issues of the first house, Mars and the Aries archetype.

SEXUALITY Mars and Pluto will delineate the soul's capacity and need to align with natural law and healthy self-expression.

The Natural Laws of Aries

When Mars and Aries are flowing in alignment with Natural Law, you will find it easy to:

- Initiate projects
- Wake up refreshed and hit the ground running
- Pioneer with fresh ideas
- Trust your instincts
- Easily express yourself

Aries and Mars in alignment with Natural Law will also be able to attract healthy balanced people into relationships. As we individuate, we often have no sense of how we are connected to the Cosmos. We may have a blind spot as to how we are actually learning to be sourceful.

This can create karmic repercussions. Aries is a pioneering energy, and has a great zest for life. Like the sprout of life emerging from the earth,

Aries is always pushing up with new life. Mars, the planet aligned with Aries and the first house of your horoscope, is a fiery, red energetic. To harness Mars is to discover right action, which is always a balance of the Aries/Libra polarity.

The Evolutionary Mantra we can use to remind ourselves goes something like this:"I have the courage to pioneer and go forward, with respect for the personal space of the others." If you find yourself self-actualizing, while also in a happy relationship with others, you may well be mastering a mature expression of Mars.

Mars and Aries are the rulers of the natural first house of the zodiac.

Once the house position and the sign of natal Mars are determined, we look at the ruling planet of the sign of Mars. To fully delineate the natal Mars, we need to know its sign, its house position, aspects and phases with other planets. These birth chart indicators reveal what we want to accomplish during this lifetime. After we align our intention with total awareness of our Mars archetypal energies, we should be more aware of the reason for our existence.

Aries starts with this need to self-assert. We begin our lives as children following our instincts and trying to "do our own thing", which is often countered by others. Later, we learn to balance the Aries/ Libra polarity by understanding the imperative to be considerate of the others' needs. But with Mars, we must first become self-starters, pioneers, always forward-moving, physically active beings.

There are two issues that need analysis with Aries. One is excessive self-assertiveness, aka selfishness. The other is not enough self-honoring. Because Aries must balance with its polarity Libra, self-honoring must be tempered with consideration for others. When it is not, Aries is considered selfish. If Aries is imbalanced and too involved in relationships, they will also avoid the self-honoring mandate. Intention is creation. Doubt is the eraser.

Pluto Mars

Evolutionary Astrologers study the phase relationship of Mars to Pluto to assess the desires the soul wishes to experience.

The phase between the two planets reveals the stage that the soul has reached and what the capacity for evolutionary momentum requires.

For example, a soul with a Pluto Mars opening trine needs to express their talent in this life. A soul with a Pluto Mars opening or closing quincunx must learn to serve the social order with humility or it may face cataclysmic experiences of humiliation.

The trine energy can be wasted if it is not responsibly focused in a way to make the world more wonderful, beautiful or useful. Pluto in Leo trining Mars in Aries might be a skier.

Mars and Pluto are related as Mars is considered to be a lower octave of Pluto. Before Pluto was discovered in 1930, Mars was considered to be the ruler of both Scorpio and Aries. In EA, we now consider Aries lessons to be about how to follow our desires (Mars) and learn to align them with the soul's desire to be one with Natural Law (Pluto).

In the multidimensional reality in which we live, the Mars-Pluto planetary energies are very involved with our self-actualization. Mars represents those desires we wish to experience in this incarnation, and Pluto represents the Soul.

So, an important element of the Mars factor in the chart is to realize self-empowerment by identifying the desires an individual has chosen to experience in order to self-actualize.

Mars and Pluto ultimately delineate our ability to co-create with the God force.

In Vastu, the Mars-Pluto dynamic is assisted by placing a Shiva and a Kali along with Garnet and Amethyst on the Mars and Pluto lines as they run through an individual's home. The app has a way to calculate these lines. This alignment of gems and Planets helps us work on the evolutionary intentions depicted by the house and aspect placements of these two Planets.

The Devic energies of Aries remind me of the little sprout pushing up through the ground and becoming a part of my garden's life. A tomato Deva appeared to me, so bright and red and so exuberant that he had a big flowering bush of tomato buds, and we knew we were going to have tomatoes. He was so full of joy and gratitude to the other elements and to me for the water, soil and the love, I was overwhelmed with his ecstasy. It was very humbling to me to see such a love of life. He was responsible for nurturing the life of that plant, and he had succeeded. His gratitude and joy in the face of success was awesome. This is Aries, bright, happy, lively, playful, and life-affirming.

THE PIONEERS

PLUTO IN ARIES

♇ 1

8 APR 2067 DIRECT 09:29 PM UT

27 SEPT 2067 RX 5:25 AM GMT

23 FEB 2068 DIRECT 5:05 PM GMT

PLUTO STAYS IN ARIES UNTIL 2095

PLUTO WAS IN ARIES IN 1577

The evolutionary mantra for the Pluto in The Pioneering Generation **2067—2095** is:

"I HONOR MYSELF AND OTHERS—WITH A BALANCED CONSIDERATION OF BOTH."

On the first Ingress of Pluto in Aries, Mercury and the North Node were also present in Aries and Mars was in Gemini with Venus and Neptune.

This Ingress brought us Elizabethan England's Shakespeare. Pluto in Aries also gave us the extreme beauty of language that is this combination of —Mercury Pluto North Node of the Moon, Mars and Venus conjunction Neptune—can deliver to mass consciousness.

Shakespeare brought hundreds of ancient words back into the English language including: "In my mind's eye Horatio, in my mind's eye."

As Pluto Ingresses into Aries for the final time, on 20 Jan 1579, she is alone.

The Sun is with Uranus and Mercury, and here we sit more than a millennium later reading about Shakespeare on the Internet.

The PLUTO IN ARIES GENERATION

PLUTO 1ST HOUSE

It is because of the core evolutionary lesson of needing to learn to go your own way, that we choose Pluto in the First House, heavily aspecting Mars or in Aries.

This archetype, in a negative expression, correlates with use, manipulation, ulterior motives, and selfish agendas.

The need is to learn to totally align desire with your soul, so that you are moving in the right direction in your life.

"Make haste slowly."
—Augustus

TAURUS

April 21 - May 21: Tropical Western Zodiac

May 13 - June 21: Constellation of Taurus

May 13 - June 21: Sidereal Zodiac

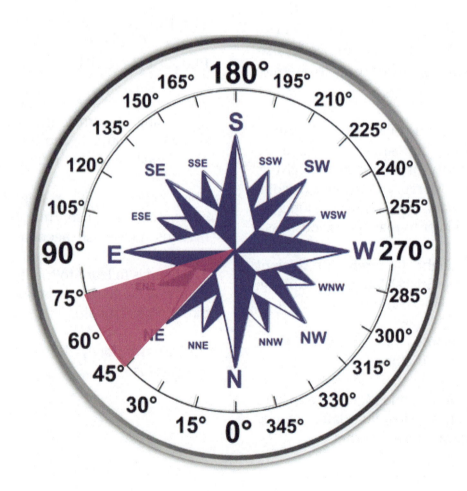

©Leigh J McCloskey, Tarot ReVisioned

DEITY

YANTRA

The Hierophant, which means priest of sacred mysteries, is the 5th key in the Tarot Arcana and is represented astrologically by the fixed earth sign Taurus.

Natural Laws of Taurus

Taurus is a member of the earth triad:

Taurus	2nd house
Virgo	6th house
Capricorn	10th house

Taurus is a member of the Fixed/Succedent Houses:

Taurus	2nd house
Leo	5th house
Scorpio	8th house
Aquarius	11th house

Tenants of the second house take on the characteristics of Taurus.

♀ Venus is the Planetary ruler of the sign ♉ Taurus and rules the second house, the natural house of Taurus and the direction of North East.

♉ When expressed through a higher frequency of manifestation, aligned with Natural Law is patient, sensual, loyal, artistic, talented, thorough, has good self-worth, demonstrates good values as well as a strong aesthetic nature.

♉ And the 2nd house when expressed through a lower frequency of manifestation may distort as lazy, self-indulgent, greedy, short-tempered, possessive, materialistic and stubborn.

Issues of material codependence, lack of perspective, fixed values based on a "frog-in-the-well" point of view, ethics/morality that is self-serving, over-reliance on stability, leading to "stick-in-the-mud" disposition, and stagnation.

♉ Glyph of the Bull's Head with Horns.

Taurus is a fixed sign - dynamic.

Taurus is the fire element - active.

Anatomy of Taurus: Ears, Neck, Vocal chords, Thyroid gland, Tongue, Mouth, Tonsils, Throat, Lower teeth.

Planets in Houses

PLANETS in the second house or in the sign of Taurus guides us to develop our own values. Learning to trust your soul life to develop your talents will give you the necessary self-valuing to earn a livelihood based on *"following your bliss."* Our survival instinct is developed in the 2h.

☉ **SUN** This planetary pairing strengthens the self-honoring principle as it combines with beauty, self love and talent. A need to face issues of self-worth can lead you to desire material possessions, when in fact you need to self-actualize through expressing your talents.

☽ **MOON** Emotional self-reliance is strengthened by the harmony available when self-appreciation turns into expressed talent. Acquisitive by nature, you may need to learn to overcome co-dependent relationships. Women will be your friends.

☿ **MERCURY** Fueling our intention to learn and name things for ourself, this combination gives us thinking that is poetic, musical or artistically gifted. We like to use our minds here to earn money.

♀ **VENUS** here loves Nature and beauty. The capacity for talent is heightened by self-respect. Survival issues may arise to teach you that you possess the capacity to earn money with your own talents. Moderation is a virtue.

♂ **MARS** is comfortable here with the Shakti to his Shiva. Venus and Mars are our Yin/Yang. There is a great quality of endurance in this combination. Practical and determined your self worth is measured by establishing your own values.

♃ **JUPITER** and Venus are a double goodness scoop of life. The expansive, optimistic outlook of a well aspected Jupiter can lead to a well aligned perspective on the true values, especially those aligned with Natural Law.

♄ **SATURN** Philanthropists have this combination. They are able to take their family accrued wealth to serve charity. Their sense of right and wrong works well with the Venusian principle's need to establish better values. They often work together to further world issues.

♅ **URANUS** Insecurities, financial ups and downs, windfalls and other forces help you develop your unique way of earning money. Rebellion against the status quo's limitations

guide you to your talented self-expression.

♆ **NEPTUNE** here allows you to find a deep well of talent to draw from for artistic pursuits. Impractical, it is wise to find good business advisors. Recognize you are a dreamer and use it to the great good.

♇ **PLUTO** in the first house drives us to pursue our evolutionary path with a passion. Wealth on many levels of life is possible. Follow the path of the heart, since all paths lead home.

Venus in the Houses

Venus in the First House

Venus here gives us a tendency to cast everyone into our movie as an underpaid extra because the first house dynamically attracts relationships. Self-actualization here will involve cyclical flip flops between commitment and withdrawal. We must learn to share, free from selfish agendas. We need to develop more understanding of other peoples needs and values.

Venus in the Second House

Self-reliance is the burning, inner fixation of this Venus. Personal values are deeply symbolic of this Venus sense of purpose. The art of living requires others who share the same values. Stability at all costs comes from a deep survival instinct which can create possessiveness and materialism, which of course, will attract possessive and controlling partners.

Venus in the Third House

Self-knowledge drives Venus here. The cyclical expansion of learning, taking classes, experimenting, reading, and all outgoing behavior of positive social interactions is highlighted. This inevitably folds into an integration mode and withdrawal. When we are not listening, we will cut others off and fail to complete sentences because we are in the contraction phase. The intellect and curiosity of Gemini/3h will evolve from indiscriminate curiosity to conscious intention to study Natural Law and found in its polarity of Sagittarius.

Venus in the Fourth House

Self-reliance is needed here and is earned through progressively stabilizing emotional reactions. As they embrace their polarity, Cap/10h of self-assuredness, they learn to minimize their codependency. Inner feelings of security, safety, and stability can only be realized by taking responsibility for their inner life. Emotions must be handled responsibly for evolution to proceed.

Venus in the Fifth House

Creative self-expression is fueled by a deep need for approval and supportive feedback. If this is not received, they will often demand it in ways that create negative attention and drama. Fulfillment requires self-actualization that is positively acknowledged. Humility, romantic love, and love of the community balances the burgeoning ego to share its talents in meaningful ways.

Venus in the Sixth House

Self-analysis motivates the self-improvement crucial to evolution. Overcoming guilt/shame and guilt/anger occur through purifying the self with integrative disciples such as meditation, shamanic healing, healthy habits, and an acceptance of one's inner life. The inner doubt and criticism are a distortion and here Venus must learn to compliment and not complain, a practice of gratitude. Returning to a non-critical stance eventually results in the self vibrating at a higher frequency, and claiming the gifts of hearing and seeing and aligning with Natural Law.

Venus in the Seventh House

Listening, comparing and contrasting the self to others begins the journey of a thousand steps of social interaction/cyclical social withdrawal. With this placement, Venus needs to adapt to the social sphere of life, learning through various kinds of relationships how to live in balance.

Venus in the Eighth House

Self-examination will involve intensity, merging, and co-creating with others. A vibrational frequency of magnetism from the Soul attracts or frightens others who are not as used to the eagle-eyed perspective of Scorpio/8h. Ongoing monitoring and surveying of values, honesty, and potential threats keep this Venus focused on the meaning of their life. Inwardly rigid, they must cyclically remove over-identification with power, position, security and healing others to keep them dependent.

Venus in the Ninth House

Actualizing personal truth through finding guiding principles provides a core sense of alignment with meaning and purpose. Overcoming limiting beliefs as the Venus 9h explores Natural Law/Universal Truth is the momentum needed to evolve. Compassionate understanding for others develops the humor inherent in this placement.

Venus in the Tenth House

Often slow to communicate, relate, and connect feelings or needs, this placement requires emotional maturity and self-authority. Attraction to outer ambition and social status can hurt or help, depending on how much the Soul is able to be mature and self-empowered. The natural warmth of the earthy elements combined brings dignity and kindness that radiates a sensuality that is magnetic and inviting to others.

Venus in the Eleventh House

Rebellious and individuating, this Venus is often a cultural misfit or leader. Depending on evolution, we will find three kinds of values being evaluated with this placement: absolute withdrawal from consensus values, joining a Star Trek convention group of similar rebels, and the genius level detachment that gifts and guides a new collective norm.

Venus in the Twelfth House

Embracing the divine through valuing the Cosmos is "square one" for this Venus. Mystical, magically oriented and gifted. It is also cyclically necessary to "separate the wheat from the chaff" to overcome existential crises, social and personal disillusionment. Overcoming the collective victim/martyrdom issues is key to evolution. Compassion, forgiveness, unconditional love, and acceptance replace the negative programing and restore the Daemon Soul spirit.

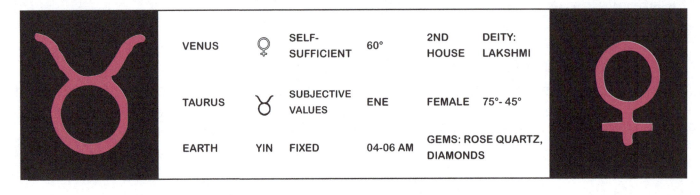

VENUS	♀	SELF-SUFFICIENT	60°	2ND HOUSE	DEITY: LAKSHMI
TAURUS	♉	SUBJECTIVE VALUES	ENE	FEMALE	75°- 45°
EARTH	YIN	FIXED	04-06 AM	GEMS: ROSE QUARTZ, DIAMONDS	

"There's a crack in everything, that is how the light gets in."
—Leonard Cohen

TAURUS KEY CONCEPTS

- Identify your talents to develop self-sufficiency.

- Learn to be self-honoring while balancing the need to be considerate of others.

- Enhance your energy to attract practical, sensual experiences.

- Magnetize abundance through self-love.

- Amplify the female energy of Venus.

- Build a foundation on Mother Earth.

"Luxury is not a matter of all the things you have, but rather all the things you can afford to live without. "
—Pico Iyer

RIGHT ACTION FOR TAURUS

DESIRES It is necessary to reflect upon what you desire. Reflect on the highest and best outcome for your life. Don't be possessive or stubborn.

GREED Harness your self-love and be open to paths that lead to both magnetism and sharing.

ACTIONS Decide your priorities and act on those impulses that fulfill your soul's desires.

SELF-WORTH In Taurus, we must trust our instincts and develop inner worth.

IDENTITY Possessiveness, self-worth, and a healthy sense of self-love are all some of the issues of the 2h Venus and Taurus.

SEXUALITY Venus and Pluto will delineate the soul's capacity and need to align with natural law and healthy self-expression.

The Natural Laws of Taurus

When Venus and Taurus are flowing in alignment with Natural Law, you will find it easy to be self-sufficient, using your talent to create a living for yourself.

Healthy self-respect is anchored in Taurus to bring your self-sustaining talents to partners, marriage, and projects and to support and nurture creative and financial endeavors.

Venus and Taurus are also very sensual and require a certain comfort from the material realm.

Taurus must refrain from over-identification with outer beauty, avoiding mirrors, and vanity periodically in order to work on inner beauty, inner truth, and inner knowing about how to align with Mother Nature.

Taurus symbolizes the need to establish emotional/psychological self-reliance and self-sufficiency.

This is accomplished through identifying our inherent capacities, and then actualizing them in a self-reliant manner.

Taurus correlates with the survival instinct, which also relates to the need to actualize the inherent capacities within the Soul. Emotional/psychological simplification will be accomplished through this process.

Taurus helps us purge all aspects of one's self that are not aligned with your true soul's essence.

As you align with this inner knowing of yourself change is no longer resisted, as it is now viewed as evolutionary momentum.

- Magnetize abundance.

- Balance your life with authentic enrichment of self and others.

- Be a generous lover, to have an abundant love life.

- Natural Law operates in Taurus through the budding of life in the Northern Hemisphere connected to the Vernal Equinox and Spring.

- As you align with the Venus/Taurus archetype, your self-worth, talent, and survival instincts develop.

- Taurus and Venus in alignment with Natural Law will also attract healthy balanced financial relationships, that involve sharing and enriching others.

"Why do we have to listen to our hearts?" the boy asked.
"Because, wherever your heart is, that is where you will find your treasure."
–Paulo Coelho

Pluto Venus

Evolutionary Astrologers study the phase relationship of Venus to Pluto to assess how well the soul is doing in rising above material concerns and stabilizing itself with Universal principles.

The Pluto/Venus phase shows how individuals can deepen self-worth by addressing issues of self-esteem. If challenging aspects are presented in the chart, we have to face the idea that atonement is the remedy.

Allowing for the possibility that we must improve our perspectives and values, JWG's EA "Frog in the Well" analogy shows a frog sitting on her lily pad and blissfully unaware that there is a vaster world above and beyond.

That "little frog" in ourselves may wish to stay in a world that can be controlled, but this is an illusion. It's a stance that enables the Pluto/Venus to avoid transformation and hold onto grudges, pout, and stay in charge of our own false narrative. In so doing, Venus/Pluto can manipulate, appropriate, and use others for self-aggrandizement.
Pluto reveals the shadow. When it connects with Venus, it reveals the necessity of developing better values. Over-accumulation of material possessions reveals deep spiritual insecurity where possessions can possess the hoarder. Venus/Pluto often needs to learn that less is more. Those who cannot share, usually are incapable of transforming their inner insecurities.

Aligning with the core Soul energy of Pluto allows us to see our interdependence with others, which is the essence of Natural Law. When Venus/Pluto is distorting our perspective and value system, we feed into the illusion of separation, and believing that power is something outside of ourselves. However, the lesson is that there is no "outside".

Venus/Taurus is about improving ourselves:
Self-sufficiency
Artistic abilities
A capacity to earn a living based on talents
Resourcefulness

Venus/Libra is about our relationships with others (see Libra/Venus/7h).

The distortion of Venus Pluto is compulsion. To overcome distortions:

- Forgive shortcomings.
- Program yourself to be kind.
- Love unconditionally, recognizing that sharing yourself lovingly will create positive changes.
- Have real conversations about unresolved relationship issues.
- Relate authentically.
- Find the origin point of Source and let it work to find your connection to All That Is.

GENERATION GODDESS PLUTO IN TAURUS

DIRECT 8 JUNE 2095 DIRECT 03:37 AM UT

RX 20 SEPTEMBER 2095 11:29 PM UT

DIRECT 22 APRIL 2096 10:21 PM UT
RX 14 NOVEMBER 2096 3:47 PM UT

PLUTO STAYS IN TAURUS UNTIL 2127
PLUTO WAS IN TAURUS IN 1851-1882

The evolutionary mantra for the Pluto in Taurus/2h/with Venus is:

" I practice self-sufficiency in practical ways while expressing my talents and sharing with others."

If you have Pluto in the second house or heavily aspecting Venus, your soul has come here to express its talent. You must learn good values of authenticity, integrity, ethics and enriching, morality and self-love.

You must give and take freely with others to help everyone with issues of trust. 2/8 polarity. If you encounter betrayal, you are simply learning to be more self-empowered.

So trust the Cosmos and pay attention to what is practical, beautiful, loving, kind, strong, magical, bountiful, and creative. Learn to earn your own living in that arena.

...with a sacred outlook, you are training yourself to be a true practitioner of human wisdom and dignity in every moment of your life."
- Guru Jagat

PLUTO IN THE SECOND HOUSE OR TAURUS

It is because of the core evolutionary lesson of needing to learn to love yourself (as you chose Pluto in Taurus) or the Second house or to have Pluto very connected/aspected to the Planet Venus

This archetype, in its negative expression, correlates with use, manipulation, and ulterior motives and selfish financial agendas. You must learn to trust yourself to earn a living and figure out who to work with, through issues of trust.

You may also be atoning for self-indulgence due to abuse of or lack of personal power.

You need to learn to have your "feet on the ground and your head in the clouds".

This connects your human values to good virtuous actions, aligned with your eternal soul and the Cosmos within you.

GEMINI

Ⅱ

May 21 - June 21: Tropical Western Zodiac

June 16 - July 16: Constellation of Gemini

June 21 - July 20: Sidereal Zodiac

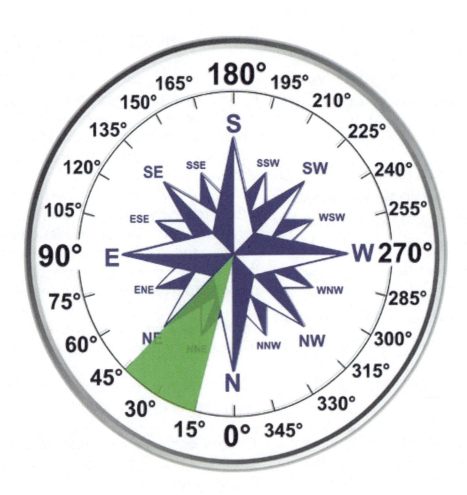

©Leigh J McCloskey, Tarot ReVisioned

MANJUSURI

YANTRA

TAROT - The Lovers - is the 6th Key in the Tarot Arcana and is represented astrologically by the mutable air sign Gemini, the twins, which is associated with communication, duality, curiosity, creativity, and intellectual dexterity.

Natural Laws of Gemini

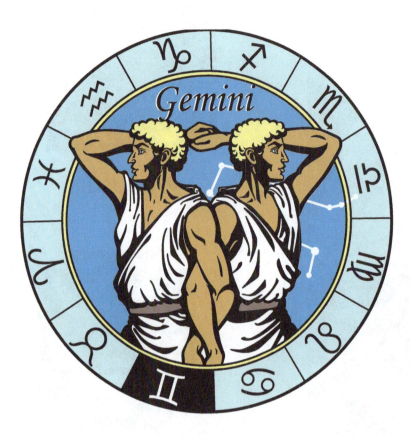

Gemini is a member of the Air Triad

Gemini	3 house Mercury
LIbra	7 house Venus
Aquarius	1 house Aquarius

Gemini is a member of the Mutable/Cadent Houses

Gemini	3rd house
Virgo	6th house
Sagittarius	9th house
Pisces	12th house

Anatomy: Arms, Shoulder, Collar Bones, Hands, Arms, Nervous System

☿ Mercury is the Planetary ruler of the sign ♊ Gemini and rules the third house, the natural house of Gemini, and the direction of North North East.

♀•♊•3rd house when expressed through a higher frequency of manifestation, aligns with Natural Law through studying, observing, and correlating, naming, and categorizing.

♊☿ and the 3rd house when expressed through a lower frequency of manifestation may distort as overly intellectual, flakey, duplicitous, and stubborn. Issues of lacking perspective, plagiarism due to being a copycat, scheming, and lying may be present.

♊ Glyph of the Twins
Gemini is a mutable sign - active.
Gemini is the air element - active.

Tenants of the third house take on the characteristics of Gemini.

Planets in Houses

ⵜ 3

PLANETS IN THE THIRD HOUSE or IN THE SIGN OF GEMINI

Planets in Gemini or in the 3rd house develop self-confidence through the ability to interpret phenomenal reality. It is here we learn languages, how to categorize and understand meaning. We are Gatherers Of Data in the sense that we want to see the whole of the Moon, the Big Picture. To achieve this objective, we must name or out-picture/projection of our inner reality. This allows us to develop an inner confidence with "manifested reality" that is aligned with our public declarations of our intentions to the universe.

☉ SUN brings the need to self-actualize to an intellectual, communications realm. Writers, teachers, thinkers, students of life. Write down your intentions.

☽ MOON combines with Mercury to make us verbally efficient at expressing our emotional life. The fluctuations of the Moon can exacerbate Gemini's "verbal diarrhea" if deep of perception isn't informing the dialogue. Feel your intentions deeply and visualize them.

☿ MERCURY is at home in Gemini's sign and house, and often excels at networking, downloading big ideas from the Cosmos, or just parroting other people's ideas. Use better word choices.

♀ VENUS in alignment with Mercury often gives a pleasing temperament. Together Venus and Mercury make us curious, amiable, and talented at learning. Use your clarity of positive words and make art.

♂ MARS is often intellectually stimulated bringing us to scientific and pioneering paths in life. Double career paths often indicated. Clarity of following up spoken words and intentions with actions is needed here.

♃ JUPITER is the polarity partner to Mercury and enhances the love of Natural Law, giving a good mind, luck, and disposition to further Daemon Soul studies. Jupiter allows you to visualize and clearly state your needs, with the highest and best good for all in the equation.

♄ SATURN harnesses time. In Gemini, it teaches us not to waste words, and makes us capable of profound depth of understanding if we seek to understand deeper subjects, like Natural Law. Use your words profoundly and with self-mastery to assist self and others.

♅ URANUS is the higher octave of Gemini, and draws the intellect up into a "Be Here Now" ability to observe the eternal present moment. It can also heighten intellectual capacity. Download ideas.

♆ NEPTUNE in the third house can extend imaginative will into the intellect. Neptune will make up words, images, ideologies, etc. You can use visualization to manifest higher energies.

♇ PLUTO in the third house a reformulation of the intellect is underway. A need to surrender intellectual prowess is required for evolution to proceed. Intensify focus on the seed you wish to grow.

MERCURY IN THE FIRST HOUSE

The desire to establish highly individual communicative skills causes these individuals to gravitate to ways of learning that promote self-discovery and innovation. The new phase of Aries/1H is attracted to new ways of learning and thinking, crucial to individuation.

MERCURY IN THE SECOND HOUSE

The mind now seeks to establish a value system that provides meaning to the overall life. Individuals with this placement are eager to define themselves through internalizing and restricting outside influences.

MERCURY IN THE THIRD HOUSE

Comfortably naming, classifying, and categorizing reality correlates to this NNE sector. Mercury is the natural ruler of the third house, so it is happy here to frame its reality with intellectual progress. Mercury here also learns to flow between its expansive learning/communicating phase and its equal need to withdraw and recapitulate.

MERCURY IN THE FOURTH HOUSE

Aligning emotional growth with intellectual growth occurs here. The need to mature will create deep emotional experiences from the choices that we make. As the mind integrates feeling and learning from these experiences, it is able to take responsibility for its co-creation with the Universe.

MERCURY IN THE FIFTH HOUSE

Creative actualization and intellectual self-expression align here with a powerful desire to fulfill a special purpose. The creative principle will be the focus of the mind. The need for recognition will create a contender for fame. Making your gifts socially relevant brings the evolutionary momentum that is needed.

MERCURY IN THE SIXTH HOUSE

The mind is learning the need for humility, introspection, and analysis as well as learning to complement instead of complaining. These mental qualities develop a reflective self-awareness that prepares us to move. from a subjective focus to the objectivity of the social order ahead in Libra.

MERCURY IN THE SEVENTH HOUSE

Listening to others teaches us the principle of relativity as we compare, contrast, and determine who it is that we want in our lives. In the West, Mercury will be especially communicative as Libra/7H is part of the Air element. We "out-picture" our inner picture here, learning to balance our specific relationship needs with our need to be free to learn.

MERCURY IN THE EIGHTH HOUSE

Pluto influences Mercury to seek a deeper understanding of how to co-create with the Cosmos. In this placement of born detectives, the mind psychoanalyzes itself and others, always looking for meaning. This Mercury can uplift others through relationships and assist them with evolution through counseling.

MERCURY IN THE NINTH HOUSE

The natural polarity of Mercury is 9H/Jupiter/Sagittarius, which helps Mercury integrate all the data it collects so that it can learn how Natural Law is working. This Mercury responds with humor to the vastness of creation.

MERCURY IN THE TENTH HOUSE

Leadership skills require Mercury here to accept responsibility for what it is putting into the Sound-stream. Knowing how to use language to communicate effectively so that words bring constructive results must be tied to Natural Law.

MERCURY IN THE ELEVENTH HOUSE

Innovative, individuating, and eclectic, this Mercury wants to collaborate with others. It must free itself from conditioning and consensus thinking.

MERCURY IN THE TWELFTH HOUSE

Visionary, talented, and imaginative, Mercury here must surrender its intellect to a deep knowing. Spiritual, transcendental ideas flow from this mind that seeks to know the Universal Mind.

"THE MIND is actually consciousness which exists as an INHERENT QUALITY OF THE ENERGY. This means that the energy has a quality which is INTELLIGENCE or CONSCIOUSNESS directing it to transform. It is as if the energy is smart all by itself. When we look at the picture of the circle which contains both the energy and the Universal Mind, they are not separate. The intelligence of the consciousness is actually the energy itself."
—Jack Schwarz

MERCURY	☿	SELF-EXPRESSION	15°	3RD HOUSE	DEITY: MANJUSURI
GEMINI	♊	SUBJECTIVE LEARNING	NE	MALE	MIND
AIR	YANG	MUTABLE	02 - 04 AM	GEMS: JADE, CITRINE	

"Do I contradict myself? Very well, then I contradict myself, I am large."
– **Walt Whitman**

GEMINI KEY CONCEPTS

- Language, naming, and categorizing, assigning meaning.

- Communication, learning, clarity, and honesty.

- Delineating and improving psychological makeup.

- Aligning your thinking with Natural Law.

- Broadening your perspective.

- Say what you mean. Mean what you say. Don't say it in a mean way!

- Don't say things behind people's backs you wouldn't say to their faces.

RIGHT ACTION FOR GEMINI

DESIRES It is necessary to reflect upon what you desire. Reflect on the highest and best outcome for your life.

PERSPECTIVE Observation and correlation are the jobs of Mercury.

BELIEFS Will be challenged as the mind opens to more.

CONTRADICTIONS Are allowed as the contrapuntal juxtaposition of the Gemini/Sagittarius polarity is revealed.

SELF-EXPRESSION In Gemini we must trust our intuition and develop inner knowing.

IDENTITY The "Self" is now related to the subjective side wherein we learn to name, categorize, classify, and use logic to discern the order of the world we are navigating.

The Natural Laws of Gemini

Natural Law of Gemini—To gather information and name it as it exists in Natural Law, realizing that there is only so much the mind can grasp about the HUGE interdependent reality.

Gemini reflects the desire for emotional security based on an exaggerated intellectual construct, which leads to loss of security when new ideas must be acknowledged.

Gemini is one half of the Gemini/Sagittarius polarity.

Gemini is the subjective side wherein we learn to name, categorize, classify, and use logic to discern the order of the world we are navigating.

The Sagittarius polarity deals with Natural Law, the style in which you communicate and learn, and the truth you are uncovering.

The cyclical unfolding of Gemini requires us to gather as much data as we can hold.

Then new information arrives, creating a withdrawal and a movement back to the inner knowing of the Soul.

GEMINI is the Planetary Archetype which leads us to find our VOICE.

Gemini also helps us organize our thinking and is the energy that correlates to networking. Mantra: I gather all twelve sides of the story to share an expanded perspective with others based on Natural Law.

Geminis can be accused of talking too much. If you have this reflected in your world, then read and watch more, contemplate, and practice listening.

Being receptive to information is a way to learn to see how the Cosmos is talking to you.

The multidimensionality of existence is chatty. Angels in a realm, fairy spirits in a realm, the future in a realm, the past in a realm--all are possibilities of how the holographic universe works. The holographic project called Life is discovered with the assistance of Mercury, the mind, which is the interface with the Cosmos.

Gemini is ruled by the Planet Mercury, and like the element of Mercury, it molds and morphs to the shape of whatever it is in contact with.

Pluto Mercury

Evolutionary Astrologers study the relationship of Mercury and Pluto to assess where the soul is at with the ability to grok how the Natural Laws of the universe work.

Pluto/Mercury will also show us how well we are able to interact with others through our capacity for learning, studying, analyzing, communication, and networking.
Gemini rules the ears and hearing.

As we learn to surrender the mind to the greater mystery and to meditation, contemplation, and poetry, we create conscious evolutionary momentum.

Pluto/Mercury deepens the mind and the shadow can be wrestled and mastered. Depth of the Soul can be integrated when the mind decides to name the soul.

GEMINI'S polarity partner is SAGITTARIUS. The third and ninth houses reflect the opinions and interpretations of ideas, and phenomena. Jupiter creates the entire belief system that is sprung from the information and ideas that Gemini has woven together. Jupiter reflects the Natural Law of the Cosmos.

PLUTO IN GEMINI
DAEMON GENERATION

Pluto in Gemini 1882-1914 & 2132-2159

Pluto in aspect to Mercury or Pluto in the third house correlates to Souls who need to gather information, reveling in the act of learning as we categorize, name, assign values, and gain experiences to expand our concepts, in order to better know the world around ourself. Pluto wants to deepen our intellectual comprehension of the conceptual world, so we are learning now to integrate the mind and the emotional/soul body to feel the world.

Pluto's depth will bring cyclic cataclysms where the logical, well structured thought process flounders. These implosions guide the Soul to breakthroughs where the dichotomies that are revealed now link into a larger pattern and point to a receptivity for a new perspective.

If there is resistance to the Plutonian cyclical cataclysms, the Soul will end up feeling disconnected. The superficial gathering of data of Gemini will miss out on forming a larger perspective. Growth for Pluto/Mercury is based on aligning with new concepts, experiences, and ideas to bring the cohesive overview of Natural Law that the Sagittarius polarity offers.

It is because of the core evolutionary lesson of needing to learn through developing the intellect, this placement will put an emphasis on education. The attempt to know as much as possible makes them avid readers, and what I call "Google University degree holders". The Evolutionary Force of Pluto guides the Soul to a deeper connection to the Cosmos because the chaotic beauty of the Cosmos is not easily rationalized.

Letting go of this desire to be in control through earnest learning will be a part of the journey of allowing oneself to vibrate with the Cosmos. The confines of having to be able to explain and understand everything intellectually can lead to crisis. In Gemini, the curiosity of the vastness of knowledge will ultimately guide the soul to what Trungpa Rinpoche described as "staying in square one", with an humility and openness to experience, and as JWG teaches, to know more and more Natural Law.

This archetype in its negative expression, correlates with opinionated, arrogant souls with whose ideas and opinions we must all be in agreement with. A reformation of ideology and the need to confront rigid, limiting beliefs, ideologies, and systems of knowing is the need of Pluto in the third house/Gemini.

CANCER

June 22 - July 22: Tropical Western Zodiac

July 20 - August 10 : Constellation of Cancer

July 17 - August 16: Sidereal Zodiac

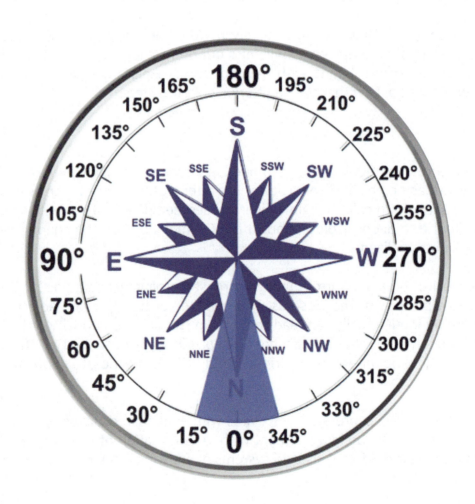

©Leigh J McCloskey,
Tarot ReVisioned

AMITABHA BUDDHA

YANTRA

The Chariot is the 7th key in the Tarot Arcana and is represented astrologically by the cardinal water sign Cancer. Cancer is associated with memory, emotion, and psychic receptivity.

Natural Laws of Cancer

"We are stardust, we are golden and we've got to get ourselves back to the garden."
- **Joni Mitchell**

Cancer is a member of the water triad:

Cancer	4th	house
Scorpio	8th	house
Pisces	12th	house

Cancer is a member of the Cardinal/Angular Houses:

Aries	1st	house
Cancer	4th	house
Libra	7th	house
Capricorn	10th	house

Tenants of the fourth house take on the characteristics of Cancer.

Moon is the ruler of the sign Cancer and rules the 4h, the natural house of Cancer, and the direction of due North.

When expressed through a higher frequency of manifestation, aligns with Natural Law through learning to be emotionally self-reliant by trusting your nature enough to trust and let go in the present moment.

And the 4h when expressing through a lower frequency of manifestation may distort as needy, co-dependent, helpless, and infantile.

Glyph of the Crab's Claw representing the spiraling of the Cosmos

Cancer is a cardinal sign - active.

Anatomy: Breasts, Chest, Stomach, Upper Lobes of the Liver

Planets in Houses

ᝪᝪ4

In the fourth house, we experience our identity as it arrives through our family of origin. This is the "DNA of the chart" and all the karma with the family or the ego's development in childhood is seen here.

⊙ SUN Self-actualization may be tied to the family history, business or legacy.

☽ MOON Emotional self-reliance will be tied to early childhood experiences as well as the relationship with one's mother and parenting.

☿ MERCURY Sensitivity allows the intellect to rest and contemplate the Cosmos, instead of always teaching, learning or talking about it.

♀ VENUS The softness of the Lunar Mansion brings out the maternal aspect of Venus. Moods will be a part of learning emotional self-reliance. Partners and parents may serve up lessons about co-dependence.

♂ MARS Empathic and sensitive, this placement allows you to feel the path forward. Making sure you have the courage to be yourself and to honor all your feelings will allow you to go forward.

♃ JUPITER Aligns us with our emotional nature, so that we can observe and correlate knowledge using feelings to know the truth.

♄ SATURN Challenges our identity to make sure it is aligned with our deepest, most sensitive feelings about the world we live in.

♅ URANUS In Cancer or the fourth house can bring instability in childhood, in order to help a soul individuate. This is a soul who is moving from level of individuation to another.

♆ NEPTUNE In the fourth house, makes a natural meditator, and a person who requires their home to be a sanctuary.

♇ PLUTO In the fourth house deepens our desire for emotional self-reliance. The burning need to connect to the soul will drive you to transform core emotional dynamics. Clearing, transforming and re-birth are all hallmarks on this journey.

MOON IN THE FIRST HOUSE

The Moon is the archetype that correlates to the development of the Ego. Here, rising in the domain of Mars/Aries/1h, the ego will experience its identity through instinctively projecting itself as a separate unique individual. The Moon will relate through experiencing its emotions in response to what comes its way, but mostly it will choose to be self-reliant and responsive to its own emotional needs, as it practices self-honoring.

MOON IN THE SECOND HOUSE

In the realm of the day ruler of Venus/Taurus/2h, the Moon is realizing the connection between its feelings and its emotional responses. As the need for self-reliance and self-sufficiency line up here, the moodiness and cyclical needs for both relating and finding security on one's own is teaching this Moon to identify with talents and resourcefulness in order to enjoy the stability of the 2h.

MOON IN THE THIRD HOUSE

Emotional security and intellectual prowess meet up here. The desire to order reality so that you feel emotionally stable creates a paradox, but the natural curiosity of the Mercury/3h/Gemini energies crave more and more knowledge. The Moon will examine the nature of the beliefs that are constantly shifting, and reach forward to experience reality fully through the mind, heart, soul, and emotion.

MOON IN THE FOURTH HOUSE

In the true North, the compass is at midnight. Asleep or burning the midnight oil, we drink deeply from the well of our soul life. Cognizant of our Ego and the need to develop a sense of self, this arena correlates to our emotional nature and how our childhood impacted us emotionally. We learn emotional self-reliance in the fourth house.

MOON IN THE FIFTH HOUSE

Our Ego is now on a journey of creative self-expression as it interacts with the 5h/Leo/Sun paradigm. If we can realize the purpose of our desire to express our talents using our will power, we will evolve and harness our Ego's strength and begin to share and serve others with our talents and generosity. Love is the keyword here.

MOON IN THE SIXTH HOUSE

The job of integrating our emotional development points our Ego into serving others. We are now breaking down our Ego and establishing our humility. We need a meditative discipline to help us integrate the awareness of what we need to outgrow. We are preparing to leave our subjective perspective behind, so we use the polarity of Pisces to transcend the Victim/Martyr paradigm.

MOON IN THE SEVENTH HOUSE

The Venus/Libra/7h position of the Moon pulls us into a variety of relationships from which we contrast and compare in order to develop our objective self. Maturity involves listening in this Western sector.

MOON IN THE EIGHTH HOUSE

Part of the water triad, the Moon resonates with the 8h/Pluto/Scorpio. The transformational nature of Pluto, ruler of the 8h, requires us to experience our compulsions, deal honestly with our attractions, and learn how to relate intimately with others. The Moon thrives here only if the Ego now surrenders to the Soul, in order to transform the patterns held in the Soul's history.

MOON IN THE NINTH HOUSE

The Moon is happy using its intuition to further the discovery of Natural Law. If it is ready to recognize the synchronicities of its daily life that help it have a deeper understanding of life, this is a light and welcome respite. As long as codependency with dogma is given up here, the expansive possibilities are very helpful to the evolutionary journey.

MOON IN THE TENTH HOUSE

Emotional maturity flowers in this arena if we have taken responsibility for what we create. In the due South, we will also wish to establish self-mastery, and therefore, use our personal authority to contribute to society. Family and ancestors affect one's feeling about one's social position.

MOON IN THE ELEVENTH HOUSE

Past life memories and traumas inherent from emotional security patterns must be overcome with the Moon placed here. The intuition will work well with the freedom of the 11h/ Uranus/AQ to speed up evolutionary intentions. This will not always be a cakewalk. Spiritual disciplines of introspection and non-attachment to outcomes are a must if the Moon is to mature and find a way to nurture and be nurtured by the community, friends or the world.

MOON IN THE TWELFTH HOUSE

The third of the water triad, Pisces, deepens empathy. The emotions must be embodied for evolution of the Soul. For example, a lack of empathy will be mirrored back to the Soul in the form of an insensitive, ungiving person showing up. Choosing to expose the contents of the subconscious, channeling, divination and other skills are linked to this placement. We must not impose escapist tendencies onto reality.

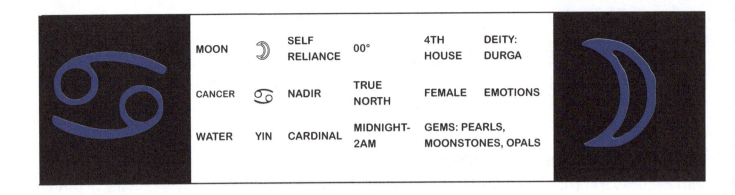

MOON	☽	SELF RELIANCE	00°	4TH HOUSE	DEITY: DURGA
CANCER	♋	NADIR	TRUE NORTH	FEMALE	EMOTIONS
WATER	YIN	CARDINAL	MIDNIGHT-2AM	GEMS: PEARLS, MOONSTONES, OPALS	

CANCER KEY CONCEPTS

- Contemplation and meditation are the evolutionary tools to connect with nature.

- Stabilize by knowing all is an inner game and one doesn't out-picture/ project one's inner life onto others.

- Amplify the female energy of the Moon with a Vedic deity of the Moon in the West to cure the Moon.

- In the Water Sign Trinity, we move through:
  Ego: Cancer, Self-Reliance
  Soul: Scorpio, Merge, Surrender
  Cosmos: Pisces, Co-create, Manifest

RIGHT ACTION FOR CANCER

DESIRES Anchor oneself deeply in one's emotional body to stabilize and be self-reliant.

EMOTIONS Find a way out of codependence by finding inner emotional security.

ACTIONS Strengthen your sense of self by overcoming submissive tendencies.

SECURITY Learn to depend on your inner emotional life.

IDENTITY Learn to harness the power of your magnetic emotional body to vibrate with the cosmos. What we vibrate is what we manifest.

SPIRITUALITY Practice direct experience of your emotions instead of metaphysical avoidance; e.g. attempting to numb yourself via meditation rather than actually confronting your life. Find your inner connection to All That Is.

The Natural Laws of Cancer

Natural Law operates in Cancer through the flowering of life in the Northern Hemisphere connected to the Summer Solstice and Summer.

To be aligned to the Moon is to feel the 2½ day cycle which delivers a very changeable, dynamic, and fluid emotional life.

The Rosicrucians teach that the Lunar archetype delivers either "lunacy, ferocity and madness" or happiness.

If the Moon energies are flowing, the individual will be highly empathetic and have good instincts, bordering on psychic awareness.

- Anchor yourself in emotional stability through a contemplative connection to your feeling nature.

- Strengthen your ego by overcoming submissive tendencies.

- Nurture yourself and your family with unconditional love.

The moon correlates to our childhood and early conditions, which imprint our whole being. Cancers like having a family, cooking, and a happy home life. Their home is their sanctuary.

The Moon involves journaling, bathing, swimming, water exercises, gardening, meditation, and prayer. The Moon lights up the Night Sky, and symbolically, this can be an energy of lighting up the subconscious mind and learning to navigate it through psychological studies, artistic expression or meditation (depending on evolutionary stages and developed gifts). It is imperative to develop one's instincts in this life and to drive all responsibility inward to develop the Moon function.

The Moon is involved with our emotional maturity. To align myself with my emotions each night before I go to sleep, I play the day backwards and look for any emotional glitches. If you find anything you wish you had reacted to differently, then send out cancel/clear energies and vow to do better under similar circumstances. I take responsibility for the entire scenario, and if I need any forgiveness— given or received— I send that prayer out as well.

Carlos Castaneda, in describing the "recapitulation" taught to him by his teacher Don Juan Matus, emphasized that one breathes from left to right as one reviews the events of the day, inhaling energy one left behind, exhaling energy one took on.

So basically, allow yourself to be like the Moon, using your intentional tides to sweep away the old and bring the new energies into yourself.

Especially allow the tides of your gratitude to flow into your life to make the changes needed to overcome difficulties, and bring new opportunities and choices your way.

PLANT WITH THE MOON

♈	Learn to: Initiate, Pioneer Excite, Enthuse
♉	Build, Use Resources, Accrue Wealth, Plan Practical pathways, Align with the organic, Earn
♊	Think, Plan, Communicate, Write, Network with others, Read, Study
♋	Nurture, Nest, Parent, Eat, Co-create with God using Intuition
♌	Play, Create, Love, Dramatize, Ennoble
♍	Analyze, Compartmentalize, Organize
♎	Socialize, Strategize, Listen, Merge, Build Partnerships, Manage Expectations
♏	Learn to Share, Change now. Intensify, Transform, Penetrate, Eliminate
♐	Travel, Study Philosophy, Study Natural Law
♑	Learn to Lead, Guide, Establish, Discriminate. Mature, Grow
♒	Build Fellowship and Strategically Align, Set Goals, Plan
♓	Envision, Dream, Meditate, Retreat, Get Cosmic

The Phases of the Moon

- New Moon: Planting—A time to begin a new project or relationship.
- First Quarter: Watering—A time to act to push forward.
- Full Moon: Blossoming—A time to reflect on what has been accomplished.
- Last Quarter: Harvesting—A time to integrate new ideas for next phase.

A lunation is a conjunction of the Sun and Moon or a New Moon. At this time, the lunar orb is seen as a thin crescent in the western sky at sunset, close to the horizon. Every night for two weeks, the lighted surface increases until it reaches the FULL phase or opposition to the Sun. Then, its light decreases for two weeks until it meets the Sun again at the next lunation. The four phases or quarters of the Moon are significant in the rise and fall of the waters on the Earth, in the rhythmic ebb and flow we call the "tides".

- The increasing Moon is the flood-tide in the affairs of humankind, strong forces for vigorous outward efforts. Good time to get acupuncture to increase energy as we are more receptive on the increasing Moon.
- The decreasing Moon or ebb-tide is for assimilating, planning, preparing, making ready for action. It is easier to calm ourselves down now.

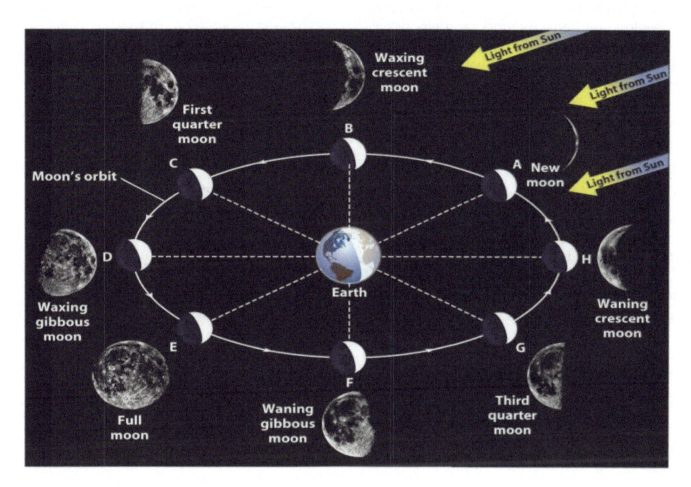

The Moon begins increasing or waxing during the 1st and 2nd quarters, at the New Moon; decreasing or waning, in theWW 3rd and 4th quarters. Whenever you can, plant when the Moon is positioned in one of the fruitful signs, Cancer, Scorpio, and Pisces; the two earth signs Taurus and Capricorn, are next in preference; also, Libra is good for flowers.

Crops that produce their yield above the soil and grow from seed with a root formation—such as beans, corn, lettuce, oats, tomatoes, sweet-peas, and marigolds—should be planted when the Moon is new or in the first quarter. Crops that produce their yield in the soil and grow from bulb formation (such as beets, carrots, potatoes, turnips, tulips, and gladiolas), should be planted when the Moon is in the full phase, especially in the last quarter.

In the last quarter of the Moon, turn sod, pull weeds, especially when the Moon is in the signs considered barren for gardening: Gemini, Leo or Virgo.

Pluto Moon

Evolutionary Astrologers study the relationship of Moon/Pluto to assess the soul's intentions to develop emotional maturity, and emotional self-reliance. We can also pinpoint how a soul will learn to connect the personal subconscious with the collective unconscious of humanity.

The Moon describes our subconscious need for inner security and Pluto demands that we also establish inner security, but it is based on our relationship with our infinite soul.

The phase relationship of Pluto & the Moon in the natal chart will reveal which evolutionary gateway the soul is working on.

The Moon supports the ego's maturity of the soul's evolution.

PLUTO/MOON Phases

• If Pluto and the Moon are in a new Phase, the soul is interested in having a fresh experience of how to ground spirituality.

• If the Soul has Moon and Pluto in an opening trine, they may be discovering creative self expression.

• If Pluto and the Moon are in a closing square the Soul has a crisis in consciousness. It is learning to widen its perception.

Positive attributes for the Moon:

Love for home and family, sensitivity, acceptance of changes in life, emotional stability, sense of responsibility, positive social behavior, attunement to the public, service to the public, ability to nurture.

Rich inner life, harmony with women.

Kindness, compassion, a sense of heritage.

Gratitude for family, ancestors, and traditions.

Negative attributes of the Moon:

Unsteadiness, moody behavior, irresponsibility, fickleness, inconsistency, excessive use of alcohol and food, bad habits.

Problematic family relations.

Emotional traumas, irrational outbursts, confusion.

Inability to nurture, lack of gratitude, insincerity, lunacy.

PLUTO IN CANCER
The Survival Generation

1914—1938
2132—2159

"I love myself as I am."

In the 4h and in the sign of Cancer, informed by the Moon, we are learning emotional self-reliance.

PLUTO IN CANCER / 4TH HOUSE

Since Cancer/Moon/4h also rule the family of origin, we are generally dealing with an evolutionary path of growth in terms of how we overcome codependence with our parents and family members.

As we learn this necessary self-sustainment we can progress smoothly or continue to cling to the herd mentality of how to fit in. Generally, "karmic necessities", will make sure that the family stability won't support a consensus, herd conditioning.

For example, a soul with this placement of Pluto will face a lot of changes, like the phases of the Moon, and learn to eventually embrace the reality of impermanence.

Resistance to change creates more and more self-reliance until true inner emotional security becomes the essence of their life. You will know when this is achieved by how little reliance one has on outer circumstances.

The generation born with Pluto in Cancer was from 1914—1938 and we called them the "Survival Generation". They suffered through the Great Depression. This time period hosted two world wars.

Cancer and Capricorn have been labeled the end of domination/submission. This generation had the Betty Crocker/ Marlboro Man syndrome according to JWG's sense of humor.

LEO

July 23 - August 23: Tropical Western Zodiac

August 10 - September 16: Constellation of Leo

August 17 - September 16: Sidereal Zodiac

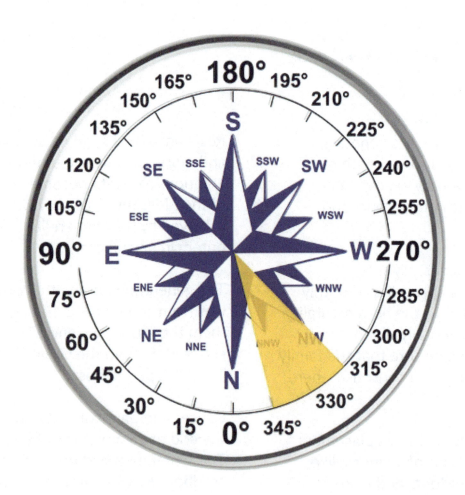

©Leigh J McCloskey, Tarot ReVisioned

Surya

YANTRA

Strength is the 8th key in the Tarot Arcana and is represented astrologically by the fixed fire sign Leo. Leo is associated with the qualities of nobility, creative self-expression and power.

Natural Laws of Leo

Leo is a member of the fire triad:

Aries   1 house
Leo   5 house
Sagittarius 9 house

Leo is a member of the Fixed/Succedent Houses:

Taurus   2nd house
Leo   5th house
Scorpio   8th house
Aquarius 11th house

Tenants of the fifth house take on the characteristics of Leo.

"All paths are the same, leading nowhere. Therefore, pick a path with heart!"
—Carlos Castaneda

The Sun is the ruler of the sign of Leo.

Rules the fifth house, the natural house of Leo, and the direction of Northwest.

When expressed through a higher frequency of manifestation, aligns with Natural Law through creative self expression. Self-actualization is the goal of this house. Intentional narcissism allows Leo to shine and share talent with others.

And the 5th house when expressing through a lower frequency of manifestation may distort proud, vain, and boastful.

Glyph of the Lion's tail.

Leo is a fixed sign - active.

Anatomy: Heart, Upper Back, Sides of the Chest

Planets in Houses

Planets in the fifth house or in the sign of Leo

It is the fifth house which is ruled by the Sun and that helps us actualize our purpose through creative self-actualization. Ruling children, romance, speculation, fun, holidays, theatre, the arts, games, hobbies, and one's avocation. We practice intentional narcissism in Leo and the fifth house in order to self-actualize through talent. We need the kudos, the appreciation, and the love. We are also learning to share love.

☉ SUN At home in the 5h, it is time to shine. Support and love are needed for the soul to grow up. The dramatic aspect of the fifth house can align with the arts.

☽ MOON Emotion and dramatic, this is a yin yang heaven and the Moon will thrive if she is given a stage, a microphone, a platform to share, care, and include.

☿ MERCURY A wild need to express creatively allows the intellect to shine and play with the Cosmos, through arts, taking a spotlight to teach or avid learning and creating from Natural Law.

♀ VENUS The Sun and Venus together are super magnetic, and the Schumann Frequency is a normal part of the brilliance of this placement. Use it to accomplish your life goals and life will be pleasant.

♂ MARS Fiery and perky, we have the fearlessness to go forward with love and appreciation for our talents and opportunities. The courage to collaborate is a test along the path.

♃ JUPITER Aligns us with our emotional nature, so that we can observe and correlate knowledge using feelings to know the truth. We may overcome obstacles easily as we rely on our Natural instincts to be one with the Cosmos. Others call this "luck".

♄ SATURN Helps us align our identity desire to makes this world a better place for all. Trusting in basic goodness allows Saturn to see the truth and beauty in romantic relationships.

♅ URANUS Here has an awakening affect on the heart. We dare to be ourselves. We dare to share our increased awareness through the arts.

♆ NEPTUNE Is the maker of visionaries and many of our filmmakers and musicians have this fifth house placement. Communicate with the world through the arts. Inspire gentleness.

♇ PLUTO In the fifth house or in LEO deepens our desire for romantic relationships. We also wish to explore our creativity at its deepest levels, and the arts create a way to share the truest secret in the Universe. Love is its very essence.

THE SUN. In our system, everything revolves around the Sun, and in our horoscope, the Sun is the center of our life. Once we understand Pluto, and our intention for incarnating, the Sun' sign and house placement shows how we want to shine.

The Sun is involved with our creativity, and in EA, the keyword is creative self-expression, and creative self-actualization. It is the focal point for actualizing the Soul's intentions. It shows us the style, actions, purpose, and the meaning of how the Soul wishes to express itself.

The house position and sign of the Sun as well as the aspects it is making to other planets describe the activities of the Soul's evolutionary expression and intention. This second of the fire signs, as well as the fifth house and the Sun's placement, describes how we will shape our lives to achieve our destiny.

Leo,The Sun, and the Fifth house also describe the special destiny we feel is ours to claim, and the entire birth chart must be examined to see how to actualize the Sun's purpose.

Find the house cusp that hosts Leo. This house is aligned with your desire to actualize the purpose of your life. That house reveals steps to self-actualize.

Leo's tarot card is the picture of Strength. The inner light from meditation fills the heart and connects us to the Cosmos. We learn to pour this heart light and love into our creativity and self-actualization.

The polarity point/Aquarius guides us to make our life socially relevant and to collaborate with others.

Our Sun sign signifies the evolutionary intention which we brought with us to Earth.

The Sun forms our unique identity: our children, education, friends, world view, the teams we support, etc.

A strongly placed Sun in the birth chart can make a person dominating, conceited, and egoistical, and this will make a person swing between feelings of insecurity and superiority. As Leo progresses toward Virgo, we find humility, especially if it we have received positive attention for our creative self-expression.

The transition from emotional self-reliance to the confidence to express oneself creatively is based on Leo's inner confidence.

We also can define our creative self expression, talents, children, and the whole gamut of the chances we will take in this life.

The ruler of the where the SUN is in the birth chart is an indicator of what we wanted to accomplish during this lifetime. We must pay very strong attention to all of the ways to delineate The Sun.

The Solstices & Ingresses of the Sun

Following its eternal path, the Sun turns around and heads back toward the equator and the Spring Equinox. This path of the Sun is called the ecliptic and all the other planets as well as the Moon follow its lead.

The other planets due to their distance and various inherent cycles, can go beyond the ecliptic. In fact, the Moon can go as far as 29° north latitude.

For the Northern Hemisphere at the Spring Equinox, the two forces of energy—yin and yang-- expansive or contractive, are in perfect balance, and therefore, the Spring equinox has been selected as the beginning of the Zodiac. It is the time identified with the realm of growth and Sunlight.

As sunlight increases, the days become longer and we approach the longest day of the year, the Summer Solstice.

The positive, expansive energies have reached their strongest peak now while the contractive, yin energy is at its lowest ebb.

The Sun then follows the ecliptic back to the equator, where the two forces are again in balance, in the sign of the Balance, Libra.

The shortest day of the year falls on the Winter Solstice, when sunlight is at its weakest.

This time of year symbolizes the more hidden realm of the value of the germinating seed. We begin our New Year on the Winter Solstice when the Sun turns at the Southern Tropic of Capricorn and heads back to the Northern Hemisphere.

In the Southern Hemisphere, these cycles are reversed. The Sun at the Southern Hemisphere turning at the Tropic of Capricorn brings Summer to the world below the equator.

"Love is like a virus. It can happen to anybody at any time."
—Maya Angelou

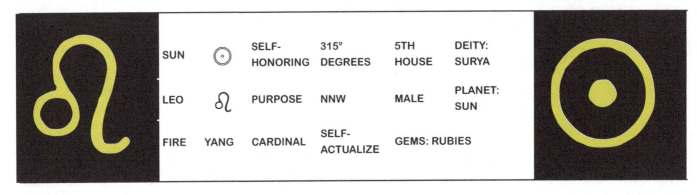

SUN	☉	SELF-HONORING	315° DEGREES	5TH HOUSE	DEITY: SURYA
LEO	♌	PURPOSE	NNW	MALE	PLANET: SUN
FIRE	YANG	CARDINAL	SELF-ACTUALIZE	GEMS: RUBIES	

"You are the Soul of the Soul of the Cosmos and your name is Love..."
– **Rumi**

LEO KEY CONCEPTS

- Love life.

- Share with all.

- Learn to be self-creating.

- Strengthen your will power.

- Shape your destiny by finding the purpose for your life.

- Vibrate the energy to attract adventures.

- Amplify the male energy of the Sun by expressing creativity.

RIGHT ACTION FOR LEO

DESIRES Exploring how to get recognition for one's talent is Leo's desire.

ANGER Leo feels it has a special destiny and gets angry if it feels someone is trying to stop its fulfillment.

CREATIVE SELF-EXPRESSION to fulfill Leo's special purpose.

STRENGTH The Soul understands that it first needs to be intentionally focused on and be full of itself in order to then reach its Aquarian polarity of disseminating and sharing its talents with others.

SEXUALITY Leo is learning to love and to integrate romance and love into their soul's journey.

"Om gaté, gaté, paragaté. parasamgaté, bodhi svaha. Gone, gone, gone beyond, gone altogether beyond, to fully awakening."
—**The Heart Sutra, Prajna Paramita Mantra**

The Natural Laws of Leo

Natural Law operates in LEO like the fruit on trees in full bloom (in the Northern Hemisphere) with our tables are full of bounty, which we can share with our friends and family, as the warm summer nights invite us to celebrate life.

The Sun is the natural ruler of Leo the Lion, and the aspect of pride, and love of family can be seen in that majestic being.

Wherever we look to the Sun, we find our sunny disposition and inner and outer romantic selves.

- Find your strength, courage and celebration.

- Unleash your talent and inner romantic self.

- Help your children, be childlike, and have fun.

- Fifth House is Sun-ruled = Find your purpose.

- Our yang energy is represented by our natal Sun. It is associated with strength and courage, and represents the basic qualities that our soul wishes to strengthen in this lifetime, in order to achieve its purpose.

Leo is the Planetary Archetype which leads us to find our HEART.

Leo also helps us express our creativity and talent, and is the energy that correlates to entertainment, acting, and managing talent as well. The tricky part for LEO is that the EGO, which was stabilized in CANCER, has now positively identified with Source–and in LEO, it learns that its talent comes from the co-creative interaction with manifest creation. The ego will take all the credit if this alignment is not actualized.

The Nemean Lion is an archetypal image of the inner powerful and savage beast within us. The "me first" attitude of this Lion can be destructive, unless tamed. We must harness our lust to preserve our creative vital instincts. Self-respect must overcome any bombastic, inflated self-importance. Strength, determination, and courage are needed to tame the ego.

As we conquer this test and engender trust in ourselves, we are loyal and act with integrity toward others. The Sun's placement in Leo or the 5h drives us to strive for fun, to be generous with our heart, and strong—all the while expressing our special purpose. Further identify your Nemean desires by the sign and house the Sun and the sign LEO occupy.

Leo identifies where and how to harness your creativity and align your personal will with Divine Will.

Celebrate and enjoy your love for life. Enhance your creative energy. Find your strength by using your heart.

SUN IN THE FIRST HOUSE

The Sun is the archetype that correlates to the purpose for living. Both Leo and Aries are yang/male energies, so here the Sun is in a stage of becoming. The contrast/comparison of the first house can be amplified by a Solar force, so that we have a strong ability to be ourself and explore the desires we have in place by enfolding others into our magnetic field.

SUN IN THE SECOND HOUSE

In the realm of the day ruler of Venus/Taurus/2h, the Sun is strengthening the resolve for self-sufficiency based on true values and not desire for material possessions or riches. Riches here have to do with what is found within that becomes abundance when shared. Highly magnetic here, the Sun can attract both wealth and happiness. The greater challenge may be to focus the talent for creative self-expression into art, avoiding the "frog-in-the-well" position of comfort.

SUN IN THE THIRD HOUSE

The Solar force is now focused on the intellect. It is observing and correlating aspects of Natural Law. Opinions and the ability to communicate are sharpened here. The relativity of the mind and the limits of the intellect are experienced. Self actualization involves linking the heart and mind, and of course as in all air signs learn to listen to facilitate conscious interactions with others.

SUN IN THE FOURTH HOUSE

In the true North, the compass is at midnight. The Sun is developing ego strength by becoming inwardly self-actualizing. Security will be realized through self-reliance. Once this is achieved the self is often directed to its 10h polarity to guide and lead others. Parenthood is a rewarding journey.

SUN IN THE FIFTH HOUSE

Our purpose is to express our romantic desires and our creative abilities so that we receive acknowledgment from the world around us. This emboldens us to overcome narcissistic tendencies as we prepare for Virgo/6h and balance the 11h polarity—both steering us to serve humanity.

SUN IN THE SIXTH HOUSE

We are now breaking down our Ego and establishing our humility. We need a meditative discipline to help us integrate the awareness of what we need to release as we prepare to leave our subjective perspective behind. Here we transcend the Victim/Martyr syndrome and learn to be of service.

SUN IN THE SEVENTH HOUSE

The Soul has reached the objective phase of evolutionary development. It desires to work on the social task of relating on a "two-way-street" with others through a series of varied and diverse relationships. Here, the purpose is to master the principle of relativity with others through learning to listen and to practice balance.

SUN IN THE EIGHTH HOUSE

The purpose of this position is to learn to merge with others, transform obsessive-compulsive disorders, and eventually to experience the larger forces of the Cosmos at work. At a level of interdependence, we will recognize how to co-create with God.

SUN IN THE NINTH HOUSE

Direct experience of Natural Law is the desire of the Sun in this arena. Correlating all the data in Gemini/3h, we then organize and make sense of it in Virgo/6h, and in Sag/9h, we discover how the Cosmos is involved in our lives.

SUN IN THE TENTH HOUSE

Strength is needed by the Sun as it is learning to establish its authority in the due South. Progressive socialization has prepared this placement of the Sun to define its special purpose through positions of authority. Self-determination is used to make sure that the ambition to succeed is made manifest. Be careful that the ends don't justify the means.

SUN IN THE ELEVENTH HOUSE

Here, the purpose of the Sun is to learn the relativity of beliefs. The strength needed here is to individuate and face that which has been outgrown. 5h/Leo is the natural polarity inviting this Sun placement to share its talents with a larger community. Innovative and rebellious, the Sun revels in its authentic self-expression.

SUN IN THE TWELFTH HOUSE

The purpose of the Solar identity here is to align with the Cosmos through something contemplative like a meditation discipline. Artistic or musical expression also strengthens the need to self actualize.

Pluto Sun

EA studies the relationship of the Sun/ Pluto to see how the Soul will self-actualize. The Leo/Aquarius polarity should be studied in order to see how the soul may share its gifts with an audience or the world.

The phase between the Sun/ Pluto describes how we are develop and express our sense of purpose.

Our yang energy is represented by the Sun in our natal horoscope. Associated with strength and courage, it is to the Sun that we look for the basic qualities that our soul wishes to express in this lifetime.

Sun/Pluto must learn to practice what Bruce Lee describes as "The art of fighting without fighting."

If Pluto is in the 5th house or strongly aspected to the Sun, you may feel you have a special destiny to bring to fruition in this life.

The combination of soul-fulfilling Pluto with the Sun helps us shape our will and use our strength to creatively self-actualize. Pluto/Sun delivers the experience of an intense inner focus. This allows us to shape our destiny and fulfill our soul's desires to align with the higher Cosmic frequency of Pluto.

Until Leo/Sun energies have been experienced through the lens of the "Bigger Picture", Leo may be very controlling. We need to practice "intentional" narcissism to get the accolades we need to find our talents, strengths, and special purpose. In this way, the subjective state of Leo evolves to learning how to serve others in Virgo.

Leo's are often guilty of entraining others into "being an underpaid extra in their Leo movie." Even the generosity of Pluto/Sun will have strings attached, until the Aquarius polarity of sharing and shared goals has been realized and balanced.

Pluto/Sun evolves as we link our unique purpose by contributing to our community. At this stage, it recognizes itself as a channel for the Cosmos.

PLUTO IN LEO
BABY BOOMERS GENERATION

7 OCT 1937 DIRECT 12:00 PM UT

25 NOVEMBER 1937 RX 9:20 AM UT

3 AUG 1938 DIRECT 6:52 PM BST

7 FEB 1939 RETROGRADE 1:03 PM UT

14 JUN 1939 DIRECT 5:42 AM BST

PLUTO STAYED IN LEO UNTIL 20 OCT 1956

The evolutionary mantra—Pluto in LEO generation
1937 - 1958

Mantra: I create with my own heart driven talents to share with my friends and community.

The evolutionary mantra—Pluto in LEO generation 1937 - 1958

Mantra: I create with my own heart driven talents to share with my friends and community.

The PLUTO IN LEO GENERATION has an AQUARIUS Pluto Polarity Point that links their destiny to a socially relevant purpose.

They are the first generation of "light workers" whose task is to build the Age of Aquarius. Many of this generation who are in the spiritual stages have this task as a core evolutionary lesson. Actualizing their purpose as a bridge builder, fulfills this special destiny. Many souls with this signature are here to strengthen future humanity for the event of Pluto entering Aquarius in 2023.

Pluto linked with Leo or the 5th house is activating the Solar force of purpose and meaning. This archetype, in a negative expression, correlates with use, manipulation, and ulterior motives and agendas. In Leo, this can lead to gambling, affairs, emotional scenes or confrontations, so they can learn to respect and see how each person is truly special.

The 5h/Leo also asks us to give birth to and raise children to be the light, talent, and the crew of the 11h/Aquarius Brotherhood.

Leo needs to learn to resonate with the strength of the Sun to shine like a lighthouse, be loved, and love and express itself creatively.

"May the long time Sun shine upon you, All Love surround you, and the Pure Light within you, Guide your way On."
—Yogi Bhajan

VIRGO

August 22 - September 23 Tropical Western Zodiac

September 16- October 30 Constellation of Virgo

September 17- October 17 Sidereal Zodiac

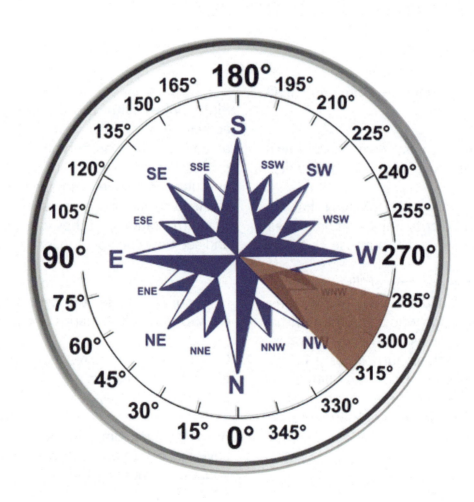

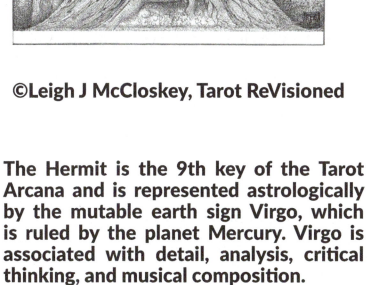

GREEN TARA

YANTRA

©Leigh J McCloskey, Tarot ReVisioned

The Hermit is the 9th key of the Tarot Arcana and is represented astrologically by the mutable earth sign Virgo, which is ruled by the planet Mercury. Virgo is associated with detail, analysis, critical thinking, and musical composition.

Natural Laws of Virgo

Virgo is a member of the earth triad:

Taurus   2nd House
Virgo   6th House
Capricorn   10 House

Virgo is a member of the Mutable/Cadent Houses:

Gemini   3rd house
Virgo   6th house
Sagittarius   9th house
Pisces   12th house

☿ Mercury is the Planetary ruler of the sign of Virgo.

♍ Virgo rules the natural house of sixth house of Virgo, and the direction of West Northwest.

♍ When expressed through a higher frequency of manifestation, aligns with Natural Law through research, good habits, learning to live in the human body, exercise, healthy routines, and integrating the first six signs of self hood.

♍ And the 6th house when expressing through a lower frequency of manifestation may distort as a Victim/Martyrdom syndrome where the pattern of guilt and shame, and guilt and anger, must be released from past lives.

♍ Glyph of the Greek word for Virgin

Virgo is a mutable sign—active.

Virgo is the earth element—passive.

Anatomy of Virgo: Intestines, Upper Bowel, Gall Bladder, Lower Solar Plexus, Liver and Pancreas.

Planets in the sixth house take on the attributes of Virgo.

Planets in Houses

Planets in the sixth house or in the sign of Virgo

Your health, habits, and the work or service that you will do in this life show up in the 6h house. Employees and employment afford some of the lessons learned by Planets tenanting this position.

The talent and self-actualization or ego development of Leo experience now moves into a need to make adjustments, so that this talent can be of service to others. EA calls this house humility or humiliation and the place where we overcome Victim/Martyr through better habits and self-respect.

☉   SUN Health, healers, and healing are part of the life-force now. Self-actualization will be linked to work and health.

☽   MOON Reflects changes in your work habits and occupation. Mothering others comes easily and you must overcome bad habits or permeable boundaries. Cooking, nursing, research all helped by this placement.

☿   MERCURY is pleasure-oriented and dramatic in Leo or the fifth house. Make sure you don't let all the attention you receive create narcissistic stances. Instead teach, write, act, instruct, and inform with love.

♀   VENUS has good healthy routines here, and gets along well with others who share them or at the very least respect them. Avoid sugar and starch for a healthier body with this position.

Remember your values and relationships need you to be very solid with good habits and the humility to choose work that lifts up yourself and others.

♂   MARS   gives you a hardworking disposition here. The desire nature of Mars/ Pluto should be analyzed to determine what work you need to align with your Soul's desires.

♃   JUPITER brings its luck and optimism to the working situation, research, health, and habits. This is a daemon soul placement allowing you to learn to live in the soul-cage while understanding the natural law of the human body.

♄   SATURN can give leadership of management roles in the work place.

♅   URANUS can bring out rebellion and innovation in the working world.

♆   NEPTUNE here makes health issues hard to pinpoint because the body is extremely sensitive to toxins. Meditation and self-reflection must be a normal part of the lifestyle of healthy habits.

♇   PLUTO asks us to clean up bad habits and learn to observe Gaia's Natural Law.

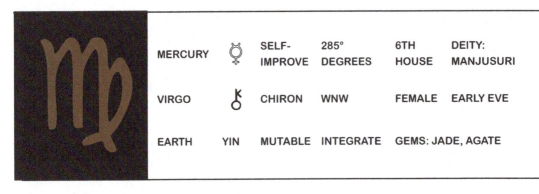

MERCURY	☿	SELF-IMPROVE	285° DEGREES	6TH HOUSE	DEITY: MANJUSURI
VIRGO	⚷	CHIRON	WNW	FEMALE	EARLY EVE
EARTH	YIN	MUTABLE	INTEGRATE	GEMS: JADE, AGATE	

"Have no fear of perfection - you'll never reach it."
- Salvador Dali

VIRGO KEY CONCEPTS

.

- Enhance your energy to attract new Angelic/Shamanistic modalities.
- Work with Angels.
- Stay active. Otherwise, paralysis and stagnation replace evolutionary effort.
- Atonement occurs through action.
- Minimalism causes Virgo to see the glass as half empty and become hypercritical.
- This critical stance derives from Virgo's basic illusion—a standard of perfection.
- Life, others, and the self always fall short of this perfectionism.
- Having painted themselves into isolation and meaninglessness—since these high illusive internal standards will never be met, Virgo fills their lives with endless activity.

RIGHT ACTION FOR VIRGO

DESIRES Reflection and integration of the aspect of the self before it becomes social.

ANGER Reflect on the highest and best outcome for your life. Abstain from criticism so as not to be criticized yourself.

RIGHT WORK It is through service that we evolve. Research, Music, Editing, Writing.

TOLERANCE Take time for yourself so that you can be fully present with others. Virgo is the polarity of Pisces; learn not to suffer nor play Victim/Martyr.

HEALING in Virgo, we learn to trust our mode of healing. Animals are often the first step.

SEXUALITY Chiron and Pluto will delineate the soul's capacity and need to align with natural healing and healthy self-expression.

The Natural Laws of Virgo

VIRGO is number 6, the 6h house, and correlates with the transition from confident, creative self-expression of talent—because it is seen as a co-creative interaction with manifest creation—to the humility to serve others.

Having lived out the LEO need to self-focus and self-inflate, as we approach Virgo, we are ready to discern how to focus the special destiny, purpose, and talents garnered through Leo. To self-improve, VIRGO must find humility and from that humility, the Natural Law of Virgo to serve others will arise.

We balance this polarity by acceptance of Source/ Natural Law, Manifested Creation, and that all cannot be known. We approach our self-improvement through steps which help us access the divine.

- Virgo is considered to be a transitional archetype. The transition is from subjective self-orientation to objective social orientation.

- From Leo, we learned to shine, and in Virgo, we learn to serve the collective and leave behind the limelight. We are overcoming shame, guilt, and Victim/Martyr as we move toward social functioning and equality.

- Virgo is the archetype of self-improvement as it focuses a high beam on what is lacking. It recognizes all imperfection and inadequacy and determines how to improve the situation.

"We must be willing to be completely ordinary people, which means accepting ourselves as we are without trying to become greater, purer, more spiritual, more insightful. If we can accept our imperfections as they are, quite ordinarily, then we can use them as part of the path. But if we try to get rid of our imperfections, then they will be enemies, obstacles on the road to our 'self-improvement'."
—**Chögyam Trungpa**

CHIRON IN THE FIRST HOUSE or in Aires ♈ 1968—1977 ☼ 2019—2026

The "Wounded Warrior" Chiron, when connecting to Mars, Aries, and the 1h is helping us restore our self-confidence. Chiron is at home in Aries, and we have pioneers and trailblazers born with this combination. They may have physical issues as well or require a great deal of physical exertion. The main goal is to become self-honoring, while balancing consideration for others.

CHIRON IN THE SECOND HOUSE or in Taurus ♉ 1977—1984 ☼ 2026—2033

Our search for value stems from wounded self-esteem. Chiron here nurtures the healing of our self-worth as we try to make sense of the material world around us. It guides us to create or earn a living that reflects our mores, ethics, and values. Examine the "frog-in-the-well" syndrome to make sure old worn-out values are not influencing your talent or inhibiting its expression.

CHIRON IN THE THIRD HOUSE or in Gemini ♊ 1983—1988 ☼ 2033—2038

Healing perception, and limiting beliefs may be a condition the Soul is facing. Using the mind to heal issues in society will be important to this soul, who is highly intuitive with a strong mind. The need to inform the greater good, influence, and manifest change are drivers in this placement. The natural curiosity of the Daemon Soul is helpful here as well.

CHIRON IN THE FOURTH HOUSE or in Cancer ♋ 1988—1991 ☼ 2038—2041

Emotional well being is forced through a series of healing crises as this soul takes the journey to self-reliance. The road map to finding inner security is the path to well-being. Outer life issues may involve helping heal the polluted, poisoned food that GMO and Glysophate additives have done to make food indigestible. Digestion is a 4h issue.

CHIRON IN THE FIFTH HOUSE or in Leo ♌ 1940—1943 ☼ 1991—1993

Our purpose, and self-actualization will heal when we practice intentional narcissism in a way that strengthens our ego so that we can express ourselves creatively. Aligned with an inner sense of purpose we must direct our ego to serve the divine. Aligning personal will with divine will is the path to healing.

CHIRON IN THE SIXTH HOUSE or in Virgo ♍ 1943—1945 ☼ 1993—1995

The Victim/Martyr syndrome is in full force in this position and we must discover how we may be of service. Distortions include workaholic tendencies and analysis/paralysis compulsion. Kundalini yoga students excel and show the higher frequency of the healing qualities of this position. The Daemon Soul is the essence of this position: shamanic healer, spiritual path finder, muse, poet, musician, naturopathic-type physician.

The "Wounded Warrior" Chiron, was discovered in 1977. I was studying with Trungpa Rinpoche, and Kalu Rinpoche, healing the wounds of a Western psyche flooded with limiting beliefs. Dharma practices and a brave new world that embraced yoga, meditation and love were the path. Little did I know then, I was part of a tribe of bridge builders who were here to enlighten a path to the New Age.

CHIRON IN THE SEVENTH HOUSE or in Libra ♎ 1944–1946 ☼ 1995–1997

A variety of relationships will be experienced that can teach the soul how to compare and contrast, and eventually, make healthy choices. Balance and harmony are the goal here. Artistic skills are present if the person has learned how to observe and correlate how they are seen by others. The path is to master the mirror of self-reflecting awareness.

CHIRON IN THE EIGHTH HOUSE or in Scorpio ♏ 1946–1948 ☼ 1997–1999

Healing obsessive-compulsive disorders is indicated by this placement of Chiron. Self empowerment lies on the other end of that scale. Learning to co-create with the Cosmos is the goal. Sexuality needs a course on Tantra. Spiritual and transformational activity such a yoga, meditation, tarot, martial arts, and astrology can help with this development.

CHIRON IN THE NINTH HOUSE or in Sagittarius ♐ 1948–1951 ☼ 1999–2001

Healing the limiting belief systems that keep the soul in an opinionated stance. Recognizing that Natural Law is at play is the goal of this placement. Once this is achieved, the soul will then begin to teach others the techniques. This is the placement of a Daemon Soul.

CHIRON IN THE TENTH HOUSE or in Capricorn ♑1951–1955 ☼ 2001–2005

This soul is learning to be self-empowered through self-mastery. Learning to be a leader requires overcoming domination/submission scenarios in the world around oneself. There will be a strong pull towards the goals of sharing, caring and inclusion.

CHIRON IN THE ELEVENTH HOUSE or in Aquarius ♒1955–1960 ☼ 2005–2011

"A thousand years of peace" is one description of the goal of mankind as we move towards the Golden Age. Those born with this position are meant to help others achieve their goals of unity and peace by guiding the way. Innovation, individuation, and freedom are needed.

CHIRON IN THE TWELFTH HOUSE or in Pisces ♓1960–1969 ☼ 2011–2019

A contemplative life that includes artistic or musical expression if talent is indicated. A meditative discipline is needed to heal the soul. The Daemon Soul chooses this position to be of inspiration to others. Woodstock happened during the 60s.

Pluto Chiron

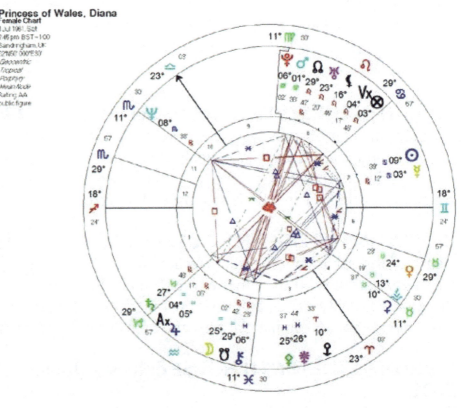

Princess of Wales, Diana
Female Chart
1 Jul 1961, Sat
7.45 pm BST -1:00
Sandringham, UK
52N50 000'E30'
Geocentric
Tropical
Placidus
Mean Node
Rating AA
public figure

Virgo is the Yin aspect of Mercury. It supports the process of receptive inward analysis and reflection. It assists us with proper judgment and critical thinking.

Chiron is the Asteroid most connected to Virgo, as both deal with healing.

Diana, Princess of Wales, has a Pluto/Chiron opposition from Chiron at 6 Pisces to Pluto at 6 Virgo.

She loomed large for a few decades as one of the most wounded women on earth because of her famously tragic marriage/divorce and death.

Her Chiron is a few minutes past Pluto putting it in the full phase, wherein she plays her life out in the objective life arena. The social arena of the full phase means she shares this wounding openly, whether she wants to or not.

The chord of Moon South Node in Aquarius conjunct Chiron reflects the experience of a detached Mother and sad childhood. It is also a possibility that the 3h placement says she will be used to teach and steer humanity away from the Victim/Martyr syndrome she found herself embodying.

The ruler of her Moon is in Leo conjunct the North Node. Pluto conjunct Mars shows us her fearless adventure-filled life as she used her REGULUS on her North Node—a fixed star associated with royalty—to shed a light on the landmines and HIV among other charities.

Generation X
Pluto in Virgo

20 OCTOBER 1956 - DIRECT-06: 09 AM UT

15 JANUARY 1957 - RX - 2: 47 AM UT

19 AUG 1957 - DIRECT- 5:21 AM BST

11 APRIL 1958 - RX - 3:02 PM UT

10 JUNE 1958 DIRECT 7:45 PM BST

PLUTO LEAVES VIRGO IN 1971

If Chiron is considered a co-ruler of Virgo, they are here to deal with healing the Planet. The Pluto Uranus conjunction in the mid-sixties began the era of revolution/evolution as Woodstock, Vietnam, Yoga, Meditation, Drugs, Rock and Roll became a part of mainstream existence.

As of this publishing in 2020 we face a world pandemic. The struggles fall on the shoulders of all the Pluto Generations. And yet it is the First Responders, Nurses, Care-Givers, Doctors and other Healers and Shamans who may be the way forward.

The protests against racial inequality is also creating a wave of revolution/evolution similar to the 60s passage of Pluto through Virgo.

Chiron squared the Nodes in the current pandemic as well as the Spanish Flu.

The evolutionary mantra for the Pluto in VIRGO generation 1956-1971 is:

"I practice being truly healthy and kind while overcoming Victim/Martyr syndromes. I analyze and integrate consistent good habits to support my radiant health."

The Pluto in Virgo generation has a core evolutionary lesson of needing to learn humility and self-improvement.

This archetype in its negative expression correlates with shame, guilt, and compulsive perfection ideologies.

Learning to get the work done instead of procrastinating leads Pluto/Virgo/6h to self-improving stances.

Developing a positive use of critical faculties along with undergoing therapy can yield awareness and growth.

What stops evolution for Virgo is paralysis due to over-analysis.

The "clean up crew" is also Pluto in Virgo.

As these folks address climate change, caused by their forefather's neglect and ignorance, these souls must forgive them, and just get on with the business of helping all.

LIBRA

September 23 - October 23: Tropical Western Zodiac

October 30- November 23: Constellation of Libra

October 31- November 16: Sidereal Zodiac

©Leigh J McCloskey, Tarot ReVisioned

JUNO

YANTRA

Justice is the 11th key in the Tarot Arcana and is represented astrologically by the cardinal air sign Libra. Libra is associated with balance, harmony, and beauty.

Natural Laws of Libra

LIBRA is a member of the a triad:

Libra   7th House
Aquarius   11th House
Gemini   3rd House

Libra is a member of the Cardinal/Angular Houses:

Libra   7th house
Capricorn 10th house
Aries   1st house
Cancer   4th house

"Truth comes by twos—in company and by opposition."
—Albert Einstein

♀   Venus is the Planetary ruler of the sign of Libra and rules the seventh house, the natural house of Libra and the direction of due WEST.

♎   When expressed through a higher frequency of manifestation that is aligned with Natural LaWw is diplomatic, a good listener, harmonious, and interested in relationships of all kinds.

♎   When expressed through a lower frequency of manifestation may project blame onto others, be unable to live on the two-way street of giving and taking. This is a sign that the maturity of consideration for others must be developed.

♎   Glyph of the Scales of Justice.

Libra is a cardinal sign—dynamic.

Libra is the air element—active.

Anatomy of Libra: Lower Back including Kidneys, Adrenal Glands, Appendix.

Tenants of the seventh house take on the characteristics of Libra.

Planets in Houses

♎ 7

Having entered the social orientation threshold at the descendant, Planets here focus us on making friends, partnerships, and a variety of people who are adept at helping us learn how to live with harmony and balance. We manage expectations in Libra and the 7h house. The circumstances of the seventh house involve business partnerships, contracts, agreements, and agents who act on your behalf, grandparents, and your attitude and ability to mature socially.

☉ **SUN** here experiences the relativity of the self, as it must let go of its willfulness, and instead learn how to maintain harmony, balance, peace, and love with others.

☽ **MOON** wishing to nurture and be nurtured, we run the risk of too many relationships. Focusing on who to trust and how to combine emotional truth with how we relate to others.

☿ **MERCURY** needs to communicate and share information so it's comfortable in the 7h or Libra.

♀ **VENUS** learns how to discriminate before jumping too far into a commitment that might tempt them to give their power to the other person.

♂ **MARS** naturally makes a passionate tenant of the 7h house or Libra, united passion and desire for unity, peace, love, sexuality, and a desire to be connected.

♃ **JUPITER** gets along with Venus so while this placement makes the material life generally easy, the real need is to use good fortune to further education in Natural Law.

♄ **SATURN** makes for a serious, profound partner. The experience of a grounded, committed relationship is crucial.

♅ **URANUS** here denotes a soul who is moving from one level on individuation to another. The Soul will be rebellious as it graduates from herd mentality in any stage of evolution. Freedom here is lived as sharing, caring and inclusion.

♆ **NEPTUNE** brings magnetism and radiance to this placement which is often channeled into visionary art, metaphysics, music or painting, dance, and all other expressions of the soul through art.

♇ **PLUTO** grounds us in this intense relationship arena to stay true to our soul's desires as we practice how to relate with others with equality, equanimity, and balance.

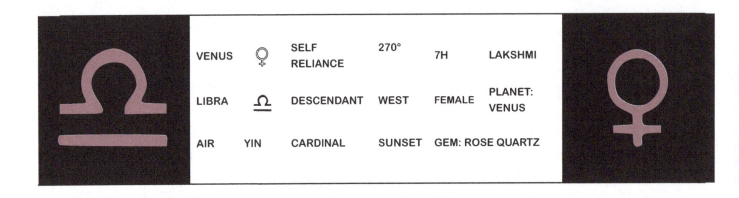

VENUS	♀	SELF RELIANCE	270°	7H	LAKSHMI
LIBRA	♎	DESCENDANT	WEST	FEMALE	PLANET: VENUS
AIR	YIN	CARDINAL	SUNSET	GEM: ROSE QUARTZ	

"Love recognizes no barriers. It jumps hurdles, leaps fences, penetrates walls to arrive at its destination full of hope." **—Maya Angelou**

LIBRA KEY CONCEPTS

- Use the talents developed in Leo and honed in Virgo to partner.

- Learn to relate to others in a balanced way.

- Enhance your energy to attract partnerships for learning.

- Magnetize partners through the love of others.

- Amplify the male energy of Venus.

- Learn through the relationships with others that we are all that is.

- We are all One.

RIGHT ACTION FOR LIBRA

DESIRE FOR RIGHT RELATIONSHIP
Having learned in Virgo to serve each other, in Libra, we learn to partner with each other.

HARNESS Your love of others to magnetize and balance all that is. Live on the two-way street.

MAGNETIZE Through sharing, caring, and love.

CONSIDERATION For yourself and others.

BALANCE Develops over a lifetime of harmonious interactions.

EXPECTATIONS Need to be managed.

DISCRIMINATE About who to love, and who to trust.

The Natural Laws of Libra

In Libra, we make a shift from a subjective to objective consciousness.

Libras initiate diverse relationships to learn the relativity that an objective, social orientation delivers.

Aries is the polarity of Libra and the balance is self-honoring with consideration for others.

We move through the romantic love of Leo and its self-absorbed viewpoint into a larger, more social experience that includes different kinds of love.

We now meet a diversity of people because we are driven in Libra to be in relationships from a codependent need for fulfillment, but we eventually learn how to be involved on an equal basis.

We mature through managing our expectations.

We recognize that we need to be loved, and we need to love.

We don't try to make it so dramatic in Libra.

We are driven towards Balance and Harmony.

We want inner and outer peace.

We learn to listen in Libra. We recognize the need for a two-way street of give-and-take.

We don't just give, nor do we just take. We find the way to have healthy interactions with consideration and self honoring acting together to make us better partners.

We evolve because we move beyond the subjective ego and all its projections and expectations.

We stay with "what is".

"Happiness is when what you think, what you say, and what you do are in harmony."
—*Mahatma Gandhi.*

Evolutionary Astrologers study the phase of Venus to Pluto to assess how the soul finds balance in relationships.

The Pluto Venus/Libra phase will also show us our objective experience—where we see ourselves the way others experience us.

The sign on the 7th house cusp describes how the others see you.

If you are not living out your own 7th house energies, you may feel like an underpaid extra in someone else's movie. This is classical Jungian projection. You must discriminate and learn who to trust, as well as who not to trust. You must learn to recognize your projections, and why you do not wish to own yourself. This stems from a lack of security, a desire to be liked, and a lazy attitude about staying in balance. This balance will be noticed by authenticity in all your interactions with others. Any ulterior motives, using of others, and lack of respect for yourself must change to consideration for yourself and others.

Libra is learning to engage with others with consideration, balancing their Aries polarity of self-honoring. In the seventh sign, and seventh house we are shifting our focus form subjectivity to objectivity.

- We move from the glory of selfhood of Leo to the service of others in Virgo into a format of equality and harmony as Libra teaches us balance. When you are using your Libra and Venus energies in alignment with Natural Law:

- Relationships flow easily and people are always attracted to you.

- You are intimate with others and you feel accepted for who you really are

- You practice balance and strive for harmony as it is key to what Libra is learning

- You are able to validate the others in your life with unconditional love and acceptance of the relationship, just as it is.

"Nature is the only true artist, and we are its apprentices."
—**Gretel Ehrlich**

Generation X
Pluto in Libra

♎ ♇ 7

5 OCT 1971—DIRECT 07: 13 AM CET17 APRIL 1972—RX 8: 51 AM BST

30 JULY 1972—DIRECT 12:37 PM BST

PLUTO LEAVES LIBRA IN 1984

The evolutionary mantra for the Pluto in Libra generation 1983-1996 is: **"I find balance in all relationships."**

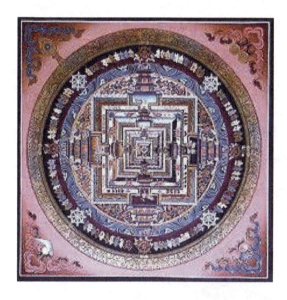

Libra must learn to listen, try out a variety of ideas, and ways of relating. Libra will compare and contrast itself to others until it overcomes the teeter-totter of extremes and desires. Eventually, Libra delivers inner harmony.

Libra is what Buddhists call "the mirror-reflecting awareness" sign, as it is about developing an understanding of projections.

The "blame game" changes when Libra learns to compliment and doesn't complain as a way of life.

The Pluto in Libra Generation is learning to walk a two-way street in how they relate with others.

They need to honor time for themselves on a regular basis. When they delve into relating to others, they are relaxed and considerate and listening to what is being reflected.

It is because of the core evolutionary lesson of needing to learn to relate with balance and equality. To minimize codependency, those in this generation will typically come into life with an emphasized need for a diversity of relationships.

This archetype, in its negative expression, correlates with giving away oneself to others. Libra, likes its Scales, must find balance and make time for itself.

All projections are self-emanating. Libras benefit greatly from analysis and can also become adept therapists.

Once one is on the road of self-empowerment, it is critical to learn which people to trust and whom not to trust.

SCORPIO

October 24 - November 22: Tropical Western Zodiac

November 23 - November 29: Constellation of Scorpio

December 17 - January 1: Constellation of Ophiuchus

October 30 - November 22: Sidereal Zodiac

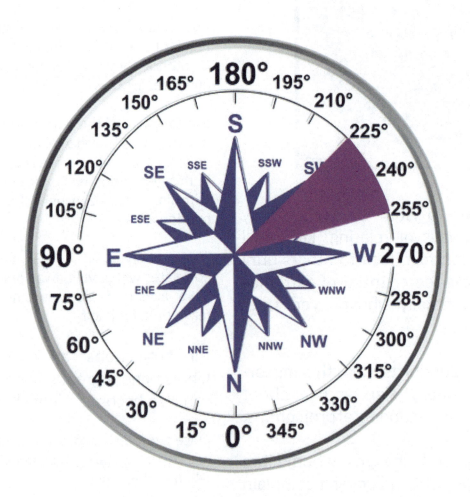

©Leigh J McCloskey, Tarot ReVisioned

DEITY

YANTRA

Death is the 13th key in the Tarot Arcana and is represented astrologically by the fixed water sign Scorpio. Scorpio is associated with hidden mysteries, the unconscious, sexual energy, and transformation.

Natural Laws of Scorpio

♇ **Pluto is the Planetary ruler of the sign Scorpio and rules the eighth house, the natural house of Scorpio and the direction of Southwest.**

♏ **When expressed through a higher frequency of manifestation is transformational, motivated to co-create with the Cosmos, penetrating, passionate, and resourceful.**

♏ **When expressed through a lower frequency of manifestation is temperamental and secretive which can create suspicion, jealousy, and intolerance. But also, Scorpio can feel untruths.**

♏ **Glyph of the Scorpion's tail.**

Scorpio is a member of the Water triad

Cancer	4th	house
Scorpio	8th	house
Pisces	12th	house

Scorpio is a member of the Fixed/Succedent Houses:

Taurus	2nd house
Leo	5th house
Scorpio	8th house
Aquarius	11th house

Anatomy of Scorpio: Genitals.

Planets in the 8h take on the characteristics of Scorpio.

"What you seek is seeking you."
—Rumi

Planets in Houses

Scorpio indicates that we are ready to learn how to merge with others and surrender in love. It is a spiritual and mystical placement, and learning to co-create with the Cosmos is a reflection of this placement's ultimate capacity. We marry, learning to cultivate inner self-empowerment. This house and sign describe the support that we receive from others, the assets of your spouse, and the inheritances you may receive. It rules surgeries, physical regeneration, death, and re-birth.

☉ SUN Strategic and needing to learn to harness power. Essentially, you are learning to co-create with the Universe.

☽ MOON The watery element here either really allows you to surrender or find yourself very stuck emotionally. You must overcome jealousy through self-empowerment. Divine timing.

☿ MERCURY The ability to see below the surface. Research, probing, and awakening the soul.

♀ VENUS Passionate, sexual, and driven. Money is a part of the path of sharing, caring, and equality, and must be used to keep the Soul in charge of the choices and partners.

♂ MARS Passionate, sexual, and pioneering. Intense, self-disciplined and trustworthy. Your desires are here to serve your soul. Marry a partner whose path is aligned with yours.

♃ JUPITER Natural Law will be learned through harnessing power and resources. The ability to co-create with the Cosmos comes from the willingness to surrender to her guidance.

♄ SATURN Magnetic, demanding, penetrating the veils between the Cosmos and her multidimensionality. Needs to overcome power as a concept outside the self in order to co-create with the Cosmos. Loyal but secretive.

♅ URANUS The freedom from the known intends to break up all that is compulsive or obsessive and bring the awareness of manifested reality into play. You can declare your intentions to the Universe, and in a twinkling of an eye, watch them manifest.

♆ NEPTUNE Consciousness is centering within the soul and surrendering the ego to align with divine will. Inner attunement through meditation, yoga, art, music, and metaphysical gifts help align you to your life's highest purpose.

♇ PLUTO Self-empowering through alignment to the soul's mission, this is a pure blast of the numinal. The passion, drive, and focus of a soulful life emerges as the surrender to co-creation with the Cosmos is realized, practiced, and owned. Distortions involved abuse of sexuality or power.

Directions

PLUTO IN THE FIRST HOUSE EAST

Pluto guides the soul. In the first house, it is a new beginning to an evolutionary intent. The need to self-actualize requires freedom to explore various desires and follow instincts. Cyclical identity crises result in a better grasp of how to make time for the self, while being considerate and listening to others.

PLUTO IN THE SECOND HOUSE

In the realm of the day ruler of Venus/Taurus/2h, Pluto is assisting the Soul to learn survival skills and engender good values. Their way of earning a living must be in sync with their evolutionary talents. Self-sufficiency results in deepening talents and leads to material wellbeing. This teaches the soul that happiness is not equated with wealth.

PLUTO IN THE THIRD HOUSE

The Soul is focused on the learning about Natural Law and correlating those discoveries to broadening its perspective on how it all vibrates together. It will learn about the relativity of the truth, embrace many philosophies, and gather information for the Soul.

PLUTO IN THE FOURTH HOUSE MIDNIGHT

In the true North, the compass is at midnight. The Sun is developing the strength of the ego, by becoming inwardly self-actualizing. Security will be realized through self-reliance.

PLUTO IN THE FIFTH HOUSE

Our Ego is now on a journey of creative self-expression. If we can realize the purpose of our desire to express our talents by using our willpower, we will evolve and harness our Ego's strength. The goal is to share and serve others with our talents and generosity. Love is the key word here.

PLUTO IN THE SIXTH HOUSE

The job of integrating our emotional development points our Ego to service as we live with humility. A meditative discipline will help us integrate the awareness of what we have outgrown. We are moving from a subjective perspective and transcending the Victim/Martyr scenario.

> "Love makes your soul crawl out from its hiding place."
> —**Zora Neale Hurston**

PLUTO IN THE SEVENTH HOUSE

As the cardinal shift to the objective phase begins, we seek balance in our relationships through listening, sharing, caring, and inclusion. A varied set of friends, partners, and casual acquaintances are the basic groundwork to contrast and compare values, and lifestyle choices. We learn consideration for the needs and wants of others.

PLUTO IN THE EIGHTH HOUSE

In its own house, Pluto takes us into deeper relationships with others. This house of marriage invites merging, surrender, and truth as the staple for intimacy. Power issues are often experienced as we transform ourselves through confrontation, truthful interaction, and eventually how to co-create with the Cosmos.

PLUTO IN THE NINTH HOUSE

The Soul is focused on the learning about how Natural Law works, and correlating those discoveries to how it can evolve. A fiery sense of special destiny continues to guide the Soul to search intuitively for its connections with the Cosmos.

PLUTO IN THE TENTH HOUSE

In the true South, the compass is at Noon and we are discovering how to take our compassionate understanding of the plight of the world into a disciplined use of our own authority as we develop the skill set of leadership.

PLUTO IN THE ELEVENTH HOUSE

Our soul now progresses through the next stage of evolution through rebellion, rejection, resistance, revolution/evolution, and innovation/invention. We are ready to find a new way forward, a new way to live, to define ourselves, and our society. As we find our uniqueness, we look for the ways to further societal goals.

PLUTO IN THE TWELFTH HOUSE

A powerful desire to connect the entire life's journey to the desires of the Soul will be the underlying theme, and naturally, this calls for a complete elimination of delusions, herd behavior, and victim/martyrdom scenarios. Evolutionary progression is the intention.

PLUTO	SELF EMPOWERMENT	240° D	8TH HOUSE	
SCORPIO	KALI	SW	VAJRA YOGINI	
WATER	YIN	FIXED	2PM-4PM	GEMS: AMETHYST

"The nature of Scorpio is penetration, not only sexually but also psychological to penetrate to the depths of their own motives, intentions, etc."
–Jeffrey Wolf Green

SCORPIO KEY CONCEPTS

- Evolution occurs naturally if we do not resist it.

- Spiritual bypassing can be an attempt to bypass the step of Cancer. We must feel ALL of the emotions that result from the desires we set in motion.

- If we avoid self-confrontation, we will not transform.

- Our natural evolutionary necessity is to feel our emotional way through life. In Scorpio, we must share our feelings and emotional states with a mate.

- Take responsibility for what you are creating and co-creation will be revealed.

- You output your inner picture. Practice honesty, authenticity, align with Natural Law.

RIGHT ACTION FOR SCORPIO

SELF-CONTAINED It is unnecessary to reflect upon the highest and best outcome for your life. Don't be self-indulgent or selfish.

POWER/POWERLESSNESS Harness your projections and instead open up the paths to personal freedom.

METAMORPHOSIS Decide on your priorities and act on the impulses that fulfill your soul's desires.

EMPOWERMENT We can learn how to co-create with the Cosmos in Scorpio. Pay attention!

VIOLATION OF TRUST Mars and Pluto will delineate the soul's capacity and need to align with Natural Law and describe healthy self-expression.

The Natural Laws of Scorpio

Scorpio is the sign that correlates to the Soul.

It is also in Scorpio that we marry, copulate, and delve into an intimacy that teaches us surrender.

This surrender expands in the spiritual state to a penetration of the Other. There, we examine our motives, intentions, our drive for power, money, sex, transformation, and confrontation. We learn we don't have to lose ourselves, we just become a part of a greater unity.

In Cancer, the first of the water triad signs, we learned emotional self-reliance. In Scorpio, the second water sign, we must overcome the fixed water aspect of Scorpio's nature—compulsiveness.

As we learn to surrender we experience a direct experience with the Cosmos. This helps us to learn self-empowerment.

Wherever Scorpio is strong in the chart,we must establish a sense of self that operates like the phoenix rising from the ashes or the cobra shedding its skin. As we change and grow, we empower a deep relationship with the Cosmos.

We will then choose partners who reflect this same desire to transform and grow as we learn how to apply this to our relationships.

To further explore your Soul's basic intention to incarnate, use the **Pluto Paradigm:**

- **Find the sign on your 8h cusp as it describes how you must learn to share with others.**
- **Study the placement of the ruler of the sign on the 8h cusp and its aspects, etc.**
- **Identify the house with Scorpio on the cusp.**
- **Identify the sign and house position of Pluto.**
- **Identify sign, house, and aspects of your Pluto in order to determine the intentions of the soul.**
- **Identify which Planets square the Nodes of the Moon as "skipped steps".**
- **Highlight the issues described by the rulers of the South and North Nodes.**
- **Study Mars by sign, house, and phase—in relationship to Pluto.**

"Three distinct creatures are used to symbolize Death's journey of transformation: the scorpion, the serpent, and the eagle. Each expresses a qualitative transition or function of the same energy. In simplest terms, the scorpion reacts, the serpent connects, and the eagle soars. "
—Leigh J. McCloskey

A Pluto Renegade

JEFFREY WOLF GREEN
2 DEC 1946 4:52 AM
HOLLYWOOD, CA

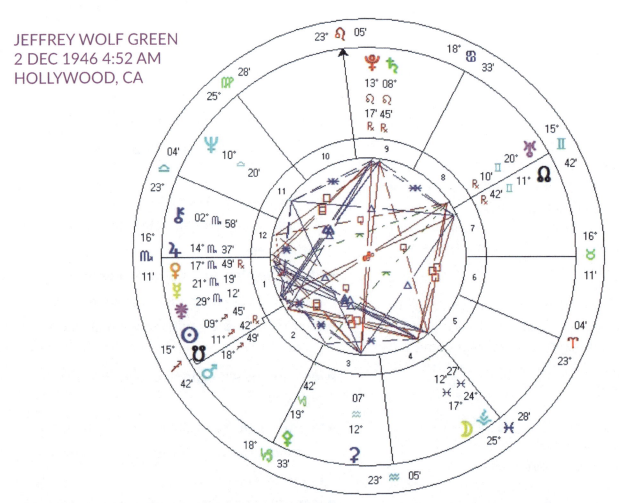

JEFFREY WOLF GREEN—THE FOUNDER OF THE SCHOOL OF EVOLUTIONARY ASTROLOGY—has Pluto Rx at 13 Leo in the 9h. His intention to align his soul and build a school is revealed by Pluto conjunct 'Saturn—the Builder'.

Scorpio is on his Ascendant, thus his self-expression is the vehicle of his Pluto, and Jupiter rises in Scorpio. Jupiter rising indicates he has traveled all over the world teaching and he `continues to educate astrologers and daemon souls who came here to help build the bridge to the Age of Aquarius.

The position of the Sun conjunct the Sun Node means he has been a world teacher already. The North Node conjunct Uranus indicates his desire to reform Astrology as it was currently guiding humanity and help give us better instructions on how to use it to evolve. Thus, he downloaded information from his multi-dimensional "friends", (Neptune in the 11th house in Libra, he seems popular in all realms.)
The ruler of the North Node is his Mercury in Scorpio and its conjunction to the ruler of his South Node, Jupiter, shows he has arrived here pretty well prepared to get this show on the road. His later withdrawal into a private life is well earned, and perhaps required by Uranus in the 8h.

81

Millenials
Pluto in Scorpio

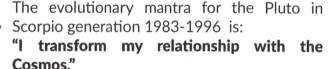

05 NOV 1983 - DIRECT - 14:06 PM EST

18 MAY 1984 - RX - 10:34 AM EDT

28 AUG 1984—DIRECT - 00:43 AM EDT

PLUTO WAS IN SCORPIO UNTIL

17 JANUARY 1995

JWG taught—Pluto in Scorpio's "inherent problem is using or manipulating others to get one's own needs met. Because the needs keep changing, typically they maintain the relationship only as long as it fulfills the current need..."
Read JWG ground breaking Evolutionary Astrology books for more insights on Pluto.

"A child is born on that day and at that hour when the celestial rays are in mathematical harmony with his or her individual karma.

The resulting horoscope is a challenging portrait revealing his or her unalterable past, and its probable future result.

But the natal chart can be rightly interpreted only by women and men of intuitive wisdom: these are few."
—Swami Sri Yukteswar

The evolutionary mantra for the Pluto in Scorpio generation 1983-1996 is:
"I transform my relationship with the Cosmos."

The Pluto in Scorpio Generation were born ready to wear their spirituality on their t-shirts. They are intense, passionate about making changes, and as they represent a huge political dynamic—are living as the change they wish to see in the world.

They are a large generation, so they are impacting government. They are also assuming, leadership of consciousness movements.

In its negative expression, this archetype correlates with using others, manipulation, ulterior motives, and agendas.

Their need to learn to co-create with the Cosmos is going to show us all how it is done.

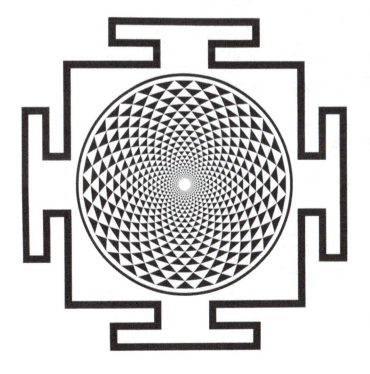

SAGITTARIUS

November 23 - December 22: Tropical Western Zodiac

December 17 - January 21: Constellation of Aries

December 17 - January 15: Sidereal Zodiac

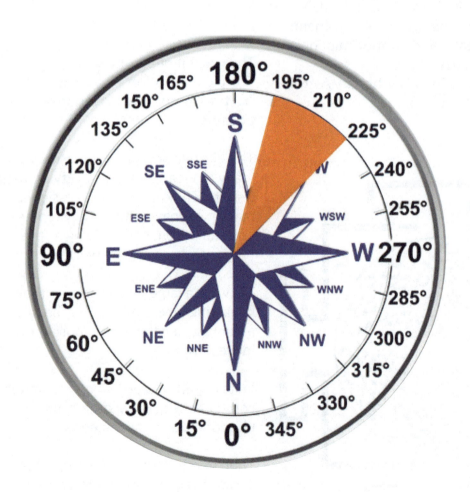

DIETY

YANTRA

©Leigh J McCloskey, Tarot ReVisioned

Temperance is the 14th key in the Tarot Arcana and is represented astrologically by the mutable fire sign Sagittarius. Sagittarius is associated with exploration, teaching, philosophy, and the innate desire for freedom.

Natural Laws of Sagittarius

**Sagittarius needs to be free.
"Don't fence me in."**

Planets in Sag and those that tenant the 9th house are under the influence of Sagittarius. Sagittarius is the third mutable sign in the mutable trinity Gemini, Virgo, Sagittarius, and Pisces. Mutable signs have adaptive qualities. Mutation, growth, evolution. Mutable signs relate to the Daemon Soul: highly intuitive, right brain dominated, in touch with Mother Nature.

 Sagittarius is a member of the fire triad

Aries	1 house
Leo	5 house
Sagittarius	9 house

⤢ Sagittarius is a member of the Cadent/Mutable houses

Gemini	3rd house
Virgo	6th house
Sagittarius	9th house
Pisces	12th house

♃ **Jupiter is the Planetary ruler of the sign Sagittarius and rules the natural ninth house, and the direction of South.**

⤢ **When expressed through a higher frequency of manifestation is humorous, unconditionally compassionate, wise, and able to teach or guide other with the principles of Natural Law.**

⤢ **When expressed through a lower frequency of manifestation is a preacher, not a teacher.**

⤢ **Glyph of the Archer's Arrow.**

Anatomy of Sagittarius: Thighs, Hips, Upper Legs.

Tenants of the ninth house take on the characteristics of Sagittarius.

Planets in Houses

Sagittarius is the place where we suspend our judgment of others, replace it with compassionate understanding and generally a sense of humor—if we are lucky.

☉ SUN This planetary pairing strengthens the self-honoring principle as is combines a fiery passion to explore Natural Law in a myriad of ways that support self-actualization.

☽ MOON Emotional self-reliance is strengthened by intuition, inner guidance. Compassionate understanding is the goal of this combination. You can stop judging self and others.

☿ MERCURY Fueling our intention to learn and name our reality, this combination gives us mental perspective. We must sink into experiential learning rather than rote memorization to "grok" Natural Law. Expanding the ability to know reality for oneself is the intention of this combination.

♀ VENUS The desire to learn, travel, and experience foreign cultures is part of the Venusian instinct. The survival instinct of Venus/Taurus now forces us to adjust our philosophical premises by correlating and contrasting religions, ideologies, values, and how best to interpret reality.

♂ MARS Expanding one's horizons to overcome the conflicting truths in human society engages Mars' ability to combat, pioneer, and brave new vistas of thought. Go forth with gentle fearlessness.

♃ JUPITER Reflects our need to explain our relationship with the Cosmos. It is the guiding force that pushes us towards an experiential relationship with the Cosmos and her Natural Laws. In its own house, Jupiter powerfully examines beliefs. Only those that inherently connect us truly and deeply to co-create with the Cosmos survive this life-long search for meaning.

♄ SATURN Puts on the brakes and forces us to examine limiting beliefs, dominating others with our beliefs or being submissive to someone else who positions their beliefs to be better than ours. Once we break out of the domination/submission paradigm, we are now free to build a better way of learning through experiencing the truth in beauty. Self-discipline must replace herd behavior for evolution to proceed.

♅ URANUS Breaks up patterns of old belief systems so that a New Day can dawn. Freedom from oppression is a part of this path towards accepting higher metaphysical truths.

♆ NEPTUNE Induces realizations about the nature of the Cosmos and all of manifested reality so that we stop thinking, philosophizing, and find a gentle inner knowing. Direct "downloads" bring the experience of the highest possible interconnectedness to All that is.

♇ PLUTO Delivers feelings of special destiny. The inner desire for complete and total alignment with Natural Law forces us beyond traditional thinking and cultural norms. Here, we find world class teachers and dedicated students of the dharma, who are determined to bypass the security of conformity. Instead, we have the desire to eliminate false beliefs, recognize limiting beliefs, and find real connection to the Cosmos that drives this train.

JUPITER	♃	FORTUNE	195°	9TH HOUSE	DEITY: GANESH
SAG	♐	NATURAL LAW	SSW	MALE	NATURAL LAW
FIRE	YANG	MUTABLE	12:00PM - 2:00 PM	GEM: TIGERS EYE	

"Sometimes, even with the most precise intuition, you don't know what life is going to throw at you. Or you could see it coming and still not be able to stave it off. That is life and part of the cycles of experience. It's not always going to be easy or fun. But with a sacred outlook, you are training yourself to be a true practitioner of human wisdom and dignity in every moment of your life."
- **Guru Jagat**

SAGITTARIUS KEY CONCEPTS

- Discover Mother Nature.

- Control intake and desire.

- Don't exaggerate, overdo or indulge.

- Truth is relative.

- Cosmic principles can be experienced.

- Confront the false beliefs of the Soul.

RIGHT ACTION FOR JUPITER

COMPASSIONATE UNDERSTANDING Truly deeply feeling the life of another leads to a gentle empathy for their condition—struggles, the drama/trauma, the places that people are stuck, the mistakes that are needed to make to us learn—are all held with compassion.

NATURAL LAW Observe and correlate the world around you. Natural Law must be realized from within.

INTUITION Arrive at knowing without needing to know why. Synchronicity unfolds when you are in the Cosmic flow.

OPEN YOUR MIND Evolve by experiencing inner knowing. Question limiting beliefs.

TEACH, DON'T PREACH Redesign your life by eliminating the need to convert others to your beliefs. Learn Natural Law by observing the Cosmic principles all around you. Teach others if they ask you to.

The Natural Laws of Sagittarius

SAGITTARIUS is number 9, the 9h. In the Sag sign and house, we begin a transition from self-empowerment, aligned with the cosmic force of our Soul to an exploration of the vaster world. Sagittarius now focuses on the relativity of the truth, as it examines limiting beliefs.

- Auspicious Beginnings.
- Lucky life, happy life.
- Protection from lesser energies.
- Make wealth your zone, seeing the wish fulfilling gem energies of Ganesh.
- Don't allow ideas to take you for a ride.
- Don't exaggerate.

Sagittarius is the study of Natural Law. We can learn to see Cosmic truth within nature. The seed cycle is an example of Natural Law. You cannot grow watermelon in a snow bank.

Overcoming limiting beliefs that are hindering evolution because they are consensus-oriented conditioned ideologies is the work of the 9th house.

Natural Law is the underlying truth of the motion of our Cosmos.

We cannot believe these truths, we must experience them directly through observing and correlation.

Sagittarius is ruled by Jupiter and involves the pursuit of knowledge, philosophy, religion, and Natural Law. We progressively learn how to grasp the vastness of the Cosmos through the sign of Sagittarius, the ninth house, and the planet Jupiter.

It is in the ninth house and through Jupiter, as well as the house cusp where we find the sign of Sagittarius in our horoscope, we are making progress with our comprehension of Natural Law. Wherever Jupiter and Sagittarius is highlighted, we are learning about our connection to the universe.

Intuition and direct experience all must replace book learning for Sagittarius. The struggle is with the intellect and the surrender needed to overcome the position that an insecure soul takes, basing its security on its ideology. These souls are busy converting others, which is indoctrination.

Sagittarius ultimately seeks a relationship with the Cosmos, and it is demonstrated by compassionate understanding and humor. Once Sagittarius takes itself past preaching, it is funny. The Cosmos is a wild ride. And Sagittarius is observing and correlating as it takes the journey. The need to understand the truth about truth drives these souls to seek freedom to explore ways of achieving a direct experience of Natural Law.

JUPITER IN THE 1ST HOUSE Expansion, progress, and exploration will drive you forward in your experience of Natural Law. Pioneering gifts are often found with this placement.

JUPITER 2ND HOUSE Broadening your values so that they are aligned with the principles of Natural Law is your soul's intention. JWG's "Frog In the Well" story informs us to leave the rabbit hole of our comfortable ideologies and examine the values and alignment with Natural Law that will take us forward.

JUPITER 3RD HOUSE At this juncture, the Soul's intellectual progress needs to confront the limits of a conventional education and delve deeper into those subjects that can overcome consensus beliefs. The goal is to develop an overarching philosophy that will provide an evolutionary spring board to a wider perspective. Travel also helps this placement of Jupiter expand a worldview.

JUPITER IN THE TRUE NORTH Connecting the emotional body to the mind, and then making sure it is secure in a relationship with the Cosmo helps the soul make progress now. Security is tied with feeling the safe harbor of family, ancestry or spiritual lineage.

JUPITER 5TH HOUSE A director at heart or an actor on the stage of life, this position evokes a playful attitude. The goal is to use creativity as the tool to develop a talent that enlightens, entertains and provokes thought.

JUPITER 6TH HOUSE A protective placement for health, here we are learning to limit our excesses and hone in on a healthier way to live in the soul-cage. Humility must be learned if we wish to avoid weight gain and health problems. Work is important, and often it is easy with this placement to find meaningful and well-paid positions.

"We can do no great things, only small things with great love."
-Mother Teresa

Directions

JUPITER - 7TH HOUSE Charismatic and deeply engaging. Here the intention is to learn objectivity and tone down rhetoric, so that we can explore relationships and exchange ideas honestly and with consideration for the other person's point of view.

JUPITER- 8TH HOUSE Deep dive into how the wheels are a turning. Expand the metaphysical connection as you develop the awareness that there are tools within your reach to co-create with the Multiverse.

JUPITER - 9TH HOUSE At home in its own house, Jupiter as the guiding evolutionary principle of Natural Law compels an expansion of understanding of the rules of the Cosmos. The relativity of beliefs is "grokked" so that a sense of humor generally reflects the synchronistic play of consciousness. Travel is another passion for this placement. Deciding what your own truth is.

JUPITER - 10TH HOUSE High honors and rewards will often ensue those who use their natural teaching or business skills to guide others from one evolutionary stage to the next. If compassionate understanding has taken root, then it is likely you will expand your ability to be a leader.

JUPITER- 11TH HOUSE
A community to both teach and learn from assures growth. Correlating and observing is the pairing of Uranus and Jupiter, so this position creates a good researcher, a good evolutionary astrologer, and a good friend to others.

JUPITER - 12TH HOUSE
Integrating relative beliefs, natural law, and ultimately experiencing the Cosmos in all its beauty and chaos are possible with this position. There is a strong protective quality reminiscent of this saying: "Fools rush in where Angels fear to tread." It must be that there is little fear because the Bigger Picture is within view.

"If you do follow your bliss you put yourself on a kind of track that has been there all the while, waiting for you, and the life that you ought to be living is the one you are living."
—Joseph Campbell

Pluto Jupiter

When Pluto and Jupiter are connected by houses, signs or aspects the Soul has decided to focus on the very nature of reality. In the consensus and individuating stage of evolution it is about the reality of Law, Wealth, and the ability to expand.

This is often found in the charts of people who have a lot of money, and they are often struggling with morality. They are learning about right attitude, aligning with their soul, and how to take right actions when earning or spending their money.

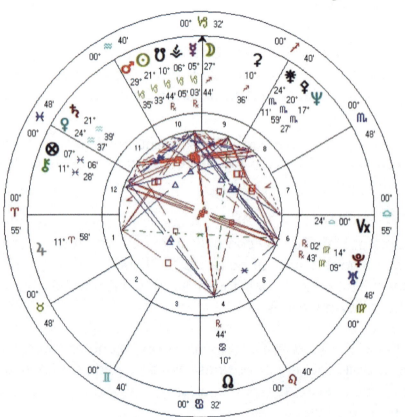

NATAL CHART OF JEFF BEZOS
- Founder of Amazon

Jeff Bezos' birth time is unavailable so we are using the 00 Aries natural wheel. He has Jupiter at 11 Aries 58 in a closing quincunx (see phases), to Uranus at 09 Virgo RX and Pluto at 14 Virgo 02 Rx.

The midpoint action at 11 Virgo creates a strong vibration between these three powerful Planets.

Jupiter is the planet of wealth and gives Bezos the pioneering spirit. Mars the ruler of Aries is at 29 Capricorn conjunct his Sun, so he is also driven to build. Uranus is the Internet. Pluto denotes the creation of e-commerce and online shopping which Bezos mastered.

Like most people born today, he has a Uranus Chiron opposition from Virgo to Pisces. Will he have lessons of Victim/Martyrdom with his employees? Most definitely. Will he find solutions for the underdog? Time will tell.

Millennials
Pluto in Sagittarius

17 JAN 1995 DIRECT 09:15 AM UT

21 APRIL 1995 3:56 AM BST

10 NOV 1995 7:11 PM UT

PLUTO WAS IN SAG UNTIL 2008

PLUTO IN THE NINTH HOUSE

Indicates a soul who knows they are connected to the Cosmos and will now be willing to go further in their own understanding of how the rules of Natural Law operate.

It is a studious position that creates our teachers, philosophers, gurus, religious fanatics, and devotees of knowledge.

These souls won't be fenced in. They need freedom to explore, identify, and often, they will also wish to teach others the forces that underly Natural Law.

This is the placement for both comedians and cosmonauts.

The evolutionary mantra for the Pluto in Sagittarius generation 1995-2008 is: **"I know I am connected to the Universe."**

The Pluto in Sagittarius Generation need to learn to live and let live. To learn to observe and correlate to experience Natural Law directly.

To use one's connectedness to all that is to help others understand Natural Law—when asked.

This archetype in its negative expression, correlates with wishing to impose your beliefs onto others.

Basing security on belief they will want to enroll others in their security blankets.

Pluto in the Ninth House denotes a Daemon Soul, and often, a truly funny person.

"The free, unhampered exchange of ideas and scientific conclusions is necessary for the sound development of science, as it is in all spheres of cultural life. ...We must not conceal from ourselves that no improvement in the present depressing situation is possible without a severe struggle; for the handful of those who are really determined to do something is minute in comparison with the mass of the lukewarm and the misguided. ...Humanity is going to need a substantially new way of thinking if it is to survive!"
—**Albert Einstein**

CAPRICORN

December 22 - January 20: Tropical Western Zodiac

January 20 - February 16: Constellation of Aries

January 16 - February 14: Sidereal Zodiac

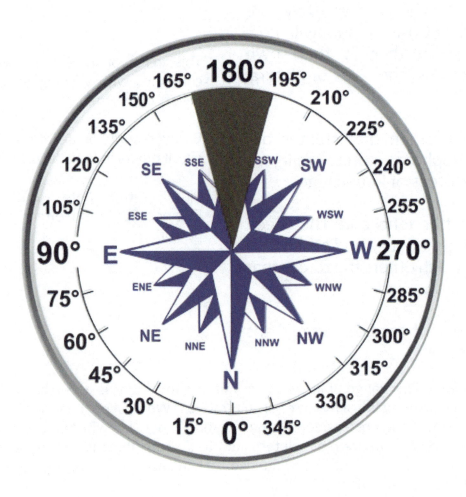

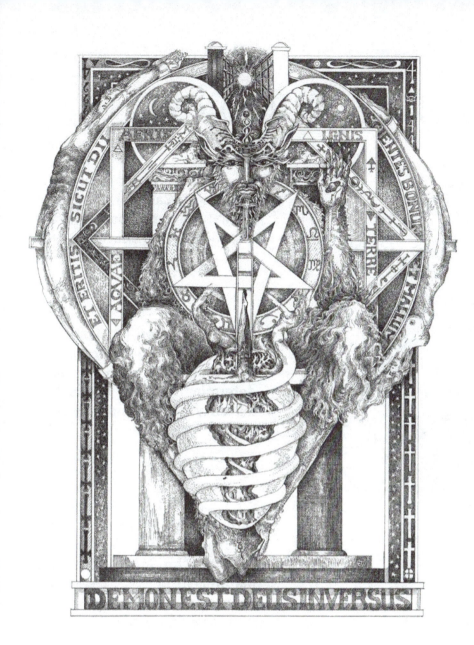

DEITY

YANTRA

©Leigh J McCloskey, Tarot ReVisioned

The Devil archetype is the 15th key in the Tarot Arcana and is represented by the cardinal earth sign Capricorn. Capricorn is ruled by the planet Saturn and is associated with limitation, restriction, earthly power, and matter

Natural Laws of CAPRICORN

Capricorn is a member of the Earth triad

Taurus	2 house
Virgo	6 house
Capricorn	10 house

Capricorn is a member of the Cardinal /Angular Houses:

Aries	1 house
Cancer	4 house
Libra	7 house
Capricorn	10 house

♄ **Saturn is the Planetary ruler of the sign Capricorn and rules the natural tenth house, and the direction of Due South.**

♑ **when expressing through a higher frequency of manifestation is self-determination, leadership, maturity, dignity, and a capacity to build.**

♑ **when expressing through a lower frequency of manifestation is "keeping up with the Jones". Dull and materialistic, repressed, suppressed, oppressed, and therefore depressed.**

♑ **Glyph of the Seagoat's Horn and Tail.**

Anatomy of Capricorn: Skin, Skeletal system, Ligaments, Knees, Gall Bladder, Parathyroid Glands, Body Protein

Tenants of the tenth house take on the characteristics of Capricorn.

10

Planets in Houses

PLANETS in the TENTH HOUSE or in the sign of CAPRICORN have reached a pinnacle of self-determination and maturity that derives from diligence and the maturity of using time wisely.

☉ SUN Self-determination is the highest frequency of this high Noon placement. If "fame" arrives, please use your inner self-mastery to guide others for the greater good for all.

☽ MOON in Capricorn or the 10th house aligns with the natural desire to nurture and enrich self and others. Here the Moon has an outlet in the world. Use it for the highest, best outcomes.

☿ MERCURY You are learning to focus your learning and speaking with increasing self-determination for success. Organized and ambitious be careful that the ends don't justify the means. Embrace dignity.

♀ VENUS The dignity of the ever-climbing Sea Goat gives us the determination to succeed at all of our endeavors. Excellence at work may give you the desire and opportunities to climb higher. Don't make status the reason for the climb, instead allow yourself to serve the Greater Good.

♂ MARS Our desire to serve our soul is well-served in this due South placement. We are working often with fame, celebrity, and influence that we need to use to guide others on the path.

♃ JUPITER Aligns our self-mastery of the principles of Nature Law into the world. We may be given opportunities to teach and guide others.

♄ SATURN Brings out the inner politician in the 10th house or Capricorn. The natural builder, producer, and self-determination you possess needs to be used to help others build shared dreams.

♅ URANUS In the house and sign of status will be an interesting roller coaster until you truly align with the collective good.

♆ NEPTUNE In the 10h gives a natural instinct of how to strategize and serve the world in a unique, visionary way.

♇ PLUTO In Capricorn or the 10h house requires us to grow up. This means to overcome domination/submission paradigms. Your soul demands worldly work.

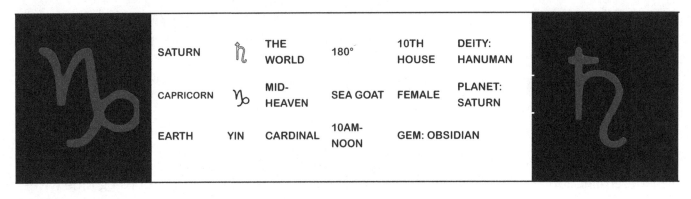

SATURN	♄	THE WORLD	180°	10TH HOUSE	DEITY: HANUMAN
CAPRICORN	♑	MID-HEAVEN	SEA GOAT	FEMALE	PLANET: SATURN
EARTH	YIN	CARDINAL	10AM-NOON		GEM: OBSIDIAN

"Let none presume to wear an undeserved dignity."
—Shakespeare

CAPRICORN KEY CONCEPTS

- Accepts responsibility.

- Uses time to honor commitments and complete life's tasks.

- Infuses morality into any status or social position in order to help guide society.

- Embraces personal authority within society to further the Greater Good.

We are moving from Capricorn into Aquarius. We are also moving from the Age of Pisces into the Age of Aquarius. We move backwards and forwards.

RIGHT ACTION FOR CAPRICORN

Those with timeless standards of conduct are inspirational to others.

They will not use devious means and they know they are responsible for their own actions. The ends do not justify the means.

DISCIPLINE Learning to be the embodiment of self-determination.

RESPONSIBILITY Using leadership abilities to do something constructive.

BOUNDARIES Limits of time and space allow us to recognize how to fulfill our destinies.

TRUTH/BEAUTY
Seeing that life is unfolding perfectly, teaching lessons of how to evolve.

AUTHORITY/MASTERY
Capricorn must learn natural leadership.

EMOTIONAL MATURITY
Overcoming Patriarchal hierarchical scenarios.

The Natural Laws of Capricorn

Saturn—Ruler of the 10th House, Capricorn and the Consensus Stage of Evolution

Saturn spends two-and-a-half years in each sign of the zodiac, and it denotes life lessons about truth, beauty, discipline, maturity, and our place in the world.

Saturn rules the consensus stage of reality, and it is the part of us that likes to fit in comfortably with others and be seen as a member of a tribe. In this stage, we want to have values that are easily understood by others.

We are good at modeling and copying the best of what we wish to achieve.

The task of Capricorn and Saturn is to practice self-determination to overcome submission to outer authority, as well as to individuate and link our social purpose to the society around us. This requires lessons of maturity.

Capricorn and Saturn in alignment with Natural Law will help you define yourself through your social function.

I like this mantra for Capricorn: **"There is no outside."** If you practice meditation and other disciplines that help you with the drive to find your inner space, and align your soul's life, then Saturn rewards you with stability because of your desire to lead others with high moral principles.

Saturn Consensus

Herd behavior. When we are not disciplined and mature we may experience inequality You like the well-trodden path and find safety in numbers, and feel like you can more readily play "the game of life" by doing what those before you have done.

Saturn Individuating

You are good at modeling and copying the best of what you yourself wish to achieve.

Rule keeper for the elite.

Producers, builders—of the new world order.

Saturn Spiritual Stages

Self-mastery to be a disciplined practitioner of the Dharma.

Stage One—New Age Teacher/Student
Stage Two—Authority & Guru
Stage Three —Inspiring Saint,
Multidimensional bridge builder.

Saturn requires discipline, self-mastery, and focusing on how much time you have in this life to accomplish those tasks you wish to accomplish.

SATURN—1ST HOUSE

Learn patience, develop a sense of timing, and look before you leap. Physical exercise is recommended. Saturn in the East is ingenious, pioneering, dynamic, and sometimes applies discipline to athletic pursuits. Saturn helps us in not spreading ourselves too thin, finding a focus, and accepting limitations.

SATURN —2ND HOUSE

It is just as important to establish an inner sense of values and personal worth as it is to have material things. Saturn here is centered and trustworthy if good values radiate self-sufficiency.

SATURN—3RD HOUSE

Learn to communicate clearly and honestly, through correlating and observing. Education is essential to develop a strong sense of identity, and the ability to learn other languages, even those such as the language of astrology, myth or archetype is sought out.

SATURN—4TH HOUSE

Saturn correlates to the 4h/10h polarity and the need to apply discipline to the development of self-reliance. It helps to not spread yourself too thin. It also amplifies the ability to find a focus and accept limitations. It is important to feel emotions with Saturn here in the due North, as well as it may be necessary to be responsible for family. Solid family values can be passed down in this area of the home.

SATURN—5TH HOUSE Some of life's lessons are to be loving and romantic, while

earning attention and respect. With Saturn here, we must guard against disappointment when others cannot shower us with approval. Instead, we must learn to be self-assured. We must express our talent and learn to have fun as we mature.

SATURN—6TH HOUSE There is a need to overcome the tendency to worry.

Encourage research, prudence, and integration as Saturn works on self-improvement while in this area. Discipline goes a long way. You will face obstacles if the Victim/Martyr scenarios are not overcome. We must forgive ourself and everyone else in order to absolve guilt and shame.

Directions

SATURN—7TH HOUSE

Lessons of managing expectations, being diplomatic, and needing to listen to others arise with Saturn in this area. Considerate, cautious, and slow to trust.

SATURN—8TH HOUSE

Learning to forgive others and to trust. Living with passion, persistence, and determination as we surrender to learning how to co-create with the Cosmos. We must take our commitments seriously. We may need to marry because we are learning to share and merge with others.

SATURN —9TH HOUSE

Here we learn to adhere to honorable and strict moral codes. A thorough education is very helpful for us to become sage, along with a commitment to study the Natural Laws of the Cosmos.

SATURN —10TH HOUSE

Develop tolerance for others. Learn to adhere to scrupulous ways of attaining goals. Living a well-organized life with a desire for self-mastery happens here. Creates responsibility and a desire to be successful. Make sure the ends don't justify the means.

SATURN—11TH HOUSE

Total freedom requires that we observe how certain rules and regulations must be followed. This level-headed attitude creates justice in the life. Investments from business pay out over the long term. A position in community wherein we are being of service to others will be rewarded.

SATURN—12TH HOUSE

Utilize imagination and creative instincts and put them into concrete form. Developing our compassionate nature so that eventually we will be empathetic and accepting. Positions of responsibility behind the scenes. Ability to be determined, disciplined, and constant will be important to health and happiness.

"You are a victim of the rules you live by."
—Jenny Holzer

Pluto Saturn

Evolutionary Astrologers study the phase relationship of Saturn to Pluto to assess the level of consensus the soul will address.

The phase between the two planets reveals the stage that the soul has reached and what the capacity for evolutionary momentum requires.

For example, a soul with a Pluto/Saturn opening quintile correlates with a need to express talent in this life. A soul with a Pluto/Saturn conjunct is learning to consolidate power.

Saturn is the need for using time effectively to achieve the goals the soul has set up in life, so the aspect between these two planets will show what kind of timing you need to master.

Pluto will work with Saturn to shape and determine ultimately how you can align with the Multiverse, and how to learn to co-create with the Cosmos.

Saturn Yantra

"The transit of Pluto through Capricorn will move over its own South Node, as well as the South Nodes of Saturn and Jupiter. It is intended to create increasingly glaring and shocking events—events that can have cataclysmic consequences due to choices made, in order to get the attention of human beings so that other choices—choices in alignment with the Natural Laws of God/dess, can be made. And those choices either way will determine, in Capricorn, how all of us will be able to live our personal lives, Cancer, on this planet: Earth. Our home..."
—JWG said this in the 1990's
www.schoolofevolutionaryastrology.com

One World
Pluto in Capricorn

♇ ⚳ 10

26 JANUARY 2008 2:37 AM UT

14 JUNE 2008 06: 13 AM BST

27 NOVEMBER 2008 01: 52 AM UT

The evolutionary mantra for the Pluto in Capricorn Generation **2008–2023** is: *"I overcome domination and submission paradigms through maturity and dignity."*

PLUTO STAYS IN CAPRICORN UNTIL MARCH 2023

PLUTO IN CAPRICORN WILL SEE THE END OF PATRIARCHAL HIERARCHAL DOMINATION SCENARIOS

PLUTO IN THE 10TH HOUSE

Warm, dignified, grounded, real, honest, true, beautiful.

These are my keywords for Capricorn at its finest. Using these qualities, Capricorn, Saturn and the tenth house are required to lead, guide, and manage the world around them, for the highest and best outcomes for all.

This generation will bring us new leaders, as the need to overcome the old paradigms expands.

Women entering political scenes is on the rise with this passage of Pluto through Capricorn.

Those with Pluto in the 10th house are here to further their self-mastery.

Pluto activating Capricorn shows the Soul is ready to takes the steps out of status based ego-driven pursuits.

The Pluto in Capricorn Generation are a part of Gen Z and there are nearly 74 million of them in the US, alone. The early ones are experiencing the confinement of a worldwide pandemic as of this writing in 2020. It will surely shape their desire to know the true inter-connectedness of the world they live in.

They equal in numbers to the Baby Boomers (76 million in the US) and the Gen X (82 million in the US).

This archetype in its negative expression, correlates with patriarchal hierarchal corruption in government, corporations, workplaces, and all top dog/bottom dog scenarios. A potential lethal virus, perhaps a biotech-weapon or the ultimate rebellion of Gaia to humanity's pollution, excess, and lack of respect for Mother Nature is delivering a powerful lesson of survival in 2020.

The need to learn self-authority, rather than giving one's authority to an outside source and then getting caught in golden handcuffs for work, prestige, fame, and leadership is a part of the Capricorn evolutionary task.

The mastery of discipline and using time effectively is another task.

AQUARIUS

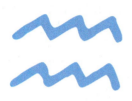

January 21 - February 18: Tropical Western Zodiac

February 15- March 15: Constellation of Aries

February 16- March 11: Sidereal Zodiac

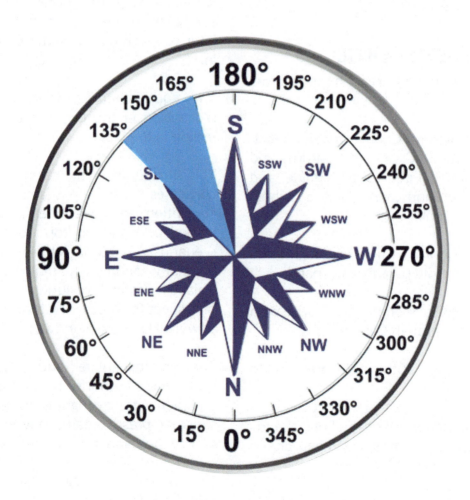

©Leigh J McCloskey, Tarot ReVisioned

SHIVA

YANTRA

The Star archetype is the 17th key of the Major Arcana of the Tarot and is represented astrologically by the fixed air sign Aquarius. Aquarius is associated with individuation, evolution, unpredictability, and genius.

Natural Laws of Aquarius

"In order to arrive at what you do not know - You must go by a way which is the way of ignorance. In order to possess what you do not possess - you must go by the way of dispossession. In order to arrive at what you are not - you must go through the way in which you are not. And what you do not know is the only thing you know. And what you own is what you do not own. And where you are is where you are not." **– T. S Eliot**

≈ Aquarius is a member of the Air triad

Gemini   3 house
Libra   7 house
Aquarius   11 house

≈ Aquarius is a member of the Fixed/ Succedent Houses:

Taurus   2 house
Leo   5 house
Scorpio   8 house
Aquarius   11 house

♅ **Uranus is the Planetary ruler of the sign Aquarius and rules the natural eleventh house, and the direction of Southeast.**

≈ **When expressed through a higher frequency of manifestation is a "rebel with a cause".**

≈ **When expressed through a lower frequency of manifestation is a "my way or the highway" person who needs to embody the Greater Good.**

≈ **Glyph of the Waterbearer's waves of light or water energy.**

Anatomy of Aquarius: Ankles, Achilles Heel.

Tenants of the eleventh house take on the characteristics of Aquarius.

Planets in Houses

11

PLANETS in the ELEVENTH HOUSE or in the sign of AQUARIUS represent the archetype of individuation, trauma, and rebellion.

Align your life goals so that helping others is a way of using your talents. Aquarian objective awareness includes —that which is above is also below—hat which is within is without. Waking up to our innate freedom happens in the 11th house.

☉ SUN This can make you very popular, especially if you are living your goals authentically. You need to choose your tribe and community carefully. Higher Love is also a goal.

☽ MOON Emotionally distant, because your self-reliance and individuation allows your to stay authentic in how your nurture yourself, others, and even the world. Learning to flow with the tides of life is liberating.

☿ MERCURY Original and resourceful in expression and popular if connected to a community who you learn from and teach. Intuitive and idealistic, you strive for authenticity in all your endeavors.

♀ VENUS The need to be different and make a difference may have to struggle to establish individuation through rebellion. May have to learn to overcome trauma/drama by aligning values with those found in Natural Law where change and impermanence are part of the cycle of life.

♂ MARS The courage to collaborate develops your ability to help everyone transcend whatever life throws our way.

♃ JUPITER The gift of friendship, education, and helping the world think outside of the box. Freedom derives through expanding perspectives.

♄ SATURN Dignified here, Saturn wants to bring technology and the future to humanity. Rebellion against conformity is necessary for evolution to proceed.

♅ URANUS Freedom from the Known. Be authentic and find your tribe. Strategical alliances are very important to all Aquarius archetypes. Rebellion against mediocrity is common here.

♆ NEPTUNE Visionary guidance to connect different levels of humanity through quantum science and the psychological, mental, physical, and spiritual mechanics behind the manifestation intention.

♇ PLUTO The Light of the Soul wants to shine as humanity learns to collaborate. If people don't learn to share, they will experience death and rebirth on many levels

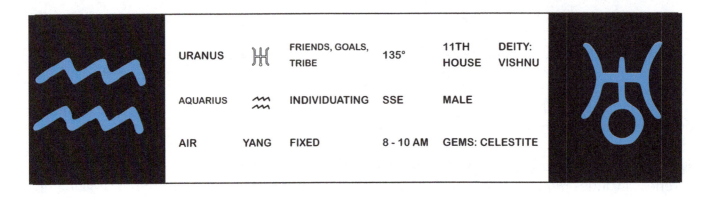

URANUS	♅	FRIENDS, GOALS, TRIBE	135°	11TH HOUSE	DEITY: VISHNU
AQUARIUS	♒	INDIVIDUATING	SSE	MALE	
AIR	YANG	FIXED	8 - 10 AM	GEMS: CELESTITE	

"Be humble for you are made of Earth, be noble for you are made of Stars."
—Serbian proverb

AQUARIUS KEY CONCEPTS

- "Freedom from the known". JWG

- Align divine will with personal will.

- Embrace impermanence.

- Find your tribe.

- Identify trauma.

- Individuation.

- Rebellion.

- Evolution/Revolution.

- Limitations of Society.

RIGHT ACTION FOR AQUARIUS

DESIRES Be Here Now. Uranus delivers us freedom from the known.

EMOTIONS Uranus teaches us to embrace impermanence as we seek to feel our way through the security of conformity to a place of authenticity.

ACTIONS Learning to liberate ourselves from limiting patterning assimilated from societal, familial, and peer pressures.

CONSIDERATION We must all learn to work and play well with others in order to survive in a group setting. This reflects the cosmic vibration of humanity as a species. As above, so below.

INDIVIDUATION Uranus vibrates the freedom from needing to conform and find security through outer values, by strengthening our individuality to allow us to be ourselves.

BREAKTHROUGHS Every time we have a download, we build dendrites in the brain. The 11/Aquarius/Uranus are related to evolution of the human brain.

The Natural Laws of Aquarius

When Uranus and Aquarius are flowing in alignment with Natural Law, you will find yourself connected to a community of like-minded souls. People demonstrating their courage to align with others who share their ideals will be the friends and colleagues of the consciously vibrating 11h Aquarius/Uranus tribe.

Natural Law operates in Aquarius through the melting of the snow and the waters that go back into to the earth to nurture the dormant seeds and feed the earth in the Northern Hemisphere —connected to the Winter.

As you align with the Uranus/Aquarius archetype, your individuality develops. You are also less attached to outcomes. The Tibetan Buddhists teach non-attachment to outcome as a way to awaken.

Aquarius and Uranus in alignment with Natural Law will also attract healthy balanced financial relationships, as the 11th house is the money you earn from your career.

Aquarius/11h/Uranus also vibrates to innovation. Contents of the collective consciousness as described by Carl Jung, himself a student of Astrology, relate to Uranus. These patterns and memories are the well spring that the soul draws upon when seeking to better understand itself.

Delving into the Uranian memories of the individuated unconscious content of the soul brings up long-term memories so that you can understand why you are doing what you are doing now, and reacting the way you do. In this way, you can liberate yourself from conditioned responses to practicing more enlightened actions to old patterns that arise.

A well-functioning Uranus creates a visionary, imaginative inventor. A poorly functioning Uranus/AQ/11h brings out elitism, snobbishness, and a disconnection from your goals, community, and leaves you functioning without the support of a "tribe."

Individuation is the goal of this archetypal frequency. To strengthen our individuality, we must cyclically disengage to overcome whatever conditioning is causing stagnation in our evolutionary growth.

Water frequency helps this Water Bearer sign, taking baths, going swimming, walking along the seaside helps the flow. Friendship and community activities are also in the purview of Uranus/AQ/11h. Take time to do things with friends, building a community spirit in your world.

Help others whenever you can. "Caring, Sharing, and Inclusion" are the keywords for Aquarius from Jeffrey Wolf Green, founder of Evolutionary Astrology.

Taking responsibility as a co-creator with God presupposes a basic understanding of how creation works. **—Carl Calleman**

URANUS IN THE FIRST HOUSE

Restless and inspired, this position of Uranus pushes and provokes more freedom at every opportunity. Thrives on change and desires breakthroughs, advances, and innovation because Uranus here correlates with new intentions for Soulful expression. Let your magic tortoise go.

URANUS IN THE SECOND HOUSE

Changes in values as the need for freedom must find resonance in how you earn a living. Many will want to be entrepreneurs if able, as working for oneself nurtures the rebellious nature that needs to tap into individuality when earning a living. There may be a desire to change societal values, but at the very least, you will have to march to the beat of your own drum.

URANUS IN THE THIRD HOUSE

Potential for brilliance if the mind is nurtured. Downloads, insights, and synchronicity all develop an adaptive intelligence that can inspire new ways of solving problems. Connecting the intellect with the intuitive mind is the goal in this position. Interruptions in formal education often occur, so that a wider scope of interests and talents are discovered.

URANUS IN THE FOURTH HOUSE

Traumas in the emotional body may surface in family scenarios. The Moon house has us spiraling up through mediation, bliss, and deep contemplation that can bring enlightening awareness. Spiraling down is a distortion of this energy because we don't assume responsibility for our feelings. The intention of the Soul is to free the self from emotional co-dependence.

URANUS IN THE FIFTH HOUSE

Tech pioneering and other creative pursuits that require being a few steps ahead of the crowd lead to a leadership position, especially if it serves the greater good. Connecting with community to share the accolades that may derive from creative self-actualization, uplifts the karma and furthers evolution.

URANUS IN THE SIXTH HOUSE

Integrating a more subtle experience of living in the soul cage. Recapitulation, meditation, Holotropic breathing, Kundalini yoga, and other spiritual practices, which are repetitive, are the path to freedom. Positive affirmations, and all other tools to liberate oneself from guilt/shame and guilt/anger.

Directions

URANUS IN THE SEVENTH HOUSE

Sharing, caring, and inclusion. Learning how to collaborate through friendship and partnerships. Integrating into a societal context creates a challenge as you find balance between your own unique desires to interact and the needs of others. Too restless to settle into any relationship conformity.

URANUS IN THE EIGHTH HOUSE

Breaking through your limitations about how your relate intimately with others ranges from conventional marriage, polyamory or Tantric initiated practices. Learning how to merge and co-create is indicated, but first, the intrinsic surrender required by tenants of this house must be met with a willingness to trust.

URANUS IN THE NINTH HOUSE

The need to leave behind outworn beliefs and ways of seeing reality will lead to a perception of Natural Law that is experiential, palpable, and even teachable with this position. Freedom to explore a diversity of ideas, philosophies, religions or other advanced ways of understanding the Cosmos must be attained.

URANUS IN THE TENTH HOUSE

If distorted, justifications are being applied to"the-ends-justifies-the means" scenarios. The intention of Uranus is to break them up. Uranus represents the ruler of the birth of the Age of Aquarius, and although not everyone with this placement is a LIGHT BRIDGE WORKER, it still represents the desire to end an old, established patriarchal order and find freedom in a social context.

URANUS IN THE ELEVENTH HOUSE

Putting ideas into action. De-conditioning from an outworn mode of living and creating alliances that build a bridge to a better life are all parts of the path out of the patriarchal hierarchal paradigms. The Soul is guiding the life through downloads of how to evolve, as well as perhaps supporting or stewarding others on the unfolding journey of birthing the Age of Aquarius. Liberation is the main theme.

URANUS IN THE TWELFTH HOUSE

"All-that-is" meets liberation from the known. Learning to Vibrate the Cosmos, and watching how it clears the path is the gift of this position. Delusion and fantasy will also be addressed as the Soul wakes up from limiting beliefs and embraces liberating interactions with the divine through meditation and other spiritual practices that no longer derive from patriarchal hierarchal or victim/martyrdom scenarios.

Pluto Uranus

Pluto and Uranus made a new phase conjunction in 1966 in Virgo. Many believe this is the beginning of the Age of Aquarius, which is still unfolding.

The Uranus and Pluto squares that lasted from 2013-2018 brought our awareness to these issues:

- How to survive without oil to look for other ways to power our cars, homes, etc.
- How to share better with each other, addressing refugees, homelessness.
- Our need for responsibility, for our planet Earth, and for our individual evolutionary path.
- Trust Mother Nature and let her teach us her mysterious ways.

- Reconsider who we share our goals with. Do they help us with our evolutionary tasks?

- Live a life that has a heartbeat. Find a real pulse from an inner life, not just the consensus-driven, material-driven, lemming life.

Uranus takes 84 years to go through all the signs, and so during that time, it will make aspects to Pluto, which will teach how to align your goals to the desires you have in your innermost soul.

You must also learn how to see your connection with your community and to somehow contribute to that tribe with your own unique creativity.

The Vibrations of Pluto and Uranus deliver an experience of a progressive loss of meaning. Our consensus beliefs block our evolution.

If we refuse to change, wake up or let go, we experience trauma/drama.

If we embrace the possibilities inherent in any challenge, we grow and evolve as we vibrate with a higher frequency of freedom. This is how we decide to wake up.

AGE OF LIGHT
PLUTO in AQUARIUS

♇ ♒ 11

23 MARCH 2023 12:14 PM UT •D

11 JUNE 2023 09:45 AM UT •RX

21 JANUARY 2024 0:50 PM UT •D

2 SEPTEMBER 2024 00: 07 AM UT •RX

19 NOVEMBER 2024 08:29 PM UT •D

PLUTO STAYS IN AQUARIUS UNTIL 2043

PLUTO IN THE 11TH HOUSE
In the realm of the ruler Uranus and the sign Aquarius, souls are looking for their tribe or community. Many will be light workers. Many will be innovators, inventors, and those who need to ditch all conditioned, herd behaviors to redefine their individuality.

If these souls are aligning with existing traditions they will generally find ways to innovate and bring it into a more collaborative, freer way of experiencing the group experience.

Evolutionary necessities of this placement include learning lessons of fight, flight or freezing as traumas are experienced. These traumas occur to break up patterns of unconscious ideation.

Detachment must be applied to arrive at an objective perspective of the ideas that shackle us. Intention is creation and the repeating of negative ideas in this house forces confrontation .

Overcome defiant use of personal will. Don't bend the will of others. Accept Universal Guidance. Collaborate.

The evolutionary mantra for the Pluto in Aquarius generation 2023–2043 is:

"I collaborate in friendship, celebrating my talent with community building, sharing happiness and love."

The Pluto in Aquarius Generation will be rebellious against the old norms of the Piscean Age. This is the generation that builds the bridge to the Age of Aquarius, assembling and using all the pieces, talents, and efforts of the light bridge worker tribes which preceded. Inventions and innovations should also break up old ways of living.

Ideally, the Aquarius frequency brings tribes together. People make friends as citizens of the same Universe. Humanity thrives and goes forth with the new structure of the Aquarian Age beginning in 2023/2024, as new technology dawns, creating a very different world.

This archetype in its negative expression, correlates with rebellion against the known, which is simply a knee-jerk reaction of nonconformity. The desire to liberate from the norm in this lifetime needs to be honored through intuitive realizations and downloads, as we learn how to vibrate with the Cosmos.

"Hearts open, Human abodes
In a world, Where no one is excluded"
—"Cyclo" Tran Anh Hung

PISCES

February 19- March 20: Tropical Pisces Western Zodiac

March 11- April 18: Constellation of Pisces

March 16- April 14: Sidereal Pisces Zodiac

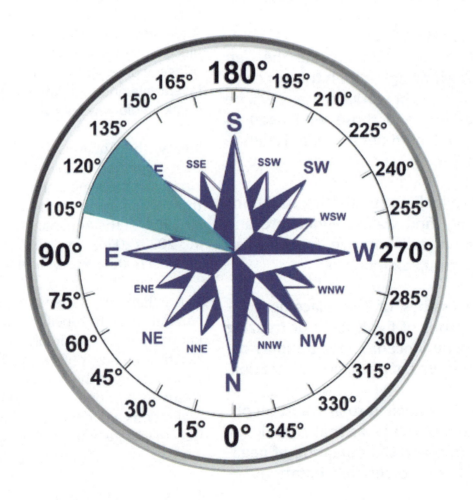

©Leigh J McCloskey, Tarot ReVisioned

KRISHNA

YANTRA

The Moon archetype is the 18th key in the Tarot Arcana and is represented astrologically by the mutable water sign Pisces. Pisces is associated with the collective unconscious, the transpersonal, dreams, unknown fears, confinement, and insanity.

Natural Laws of Pisces

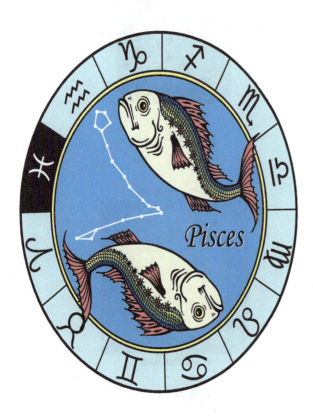

♓ Pisces is a member of the Water triad

Cancer	4th	house
Scorpio	8th	house
Pisces	12th	house

♓ Pisces is a member of the Mutable/ Cadent Houses:

Gemini	3rd house
Virgo	6th house
Sagittarius	9th house
Pisces	12th House

♆ **Uranus is the Planetary ruler of the sign Pisces and rules the natural twelfth house, and the direction of East Southeast.**

♓ **When expressed through a higher frequency of manifestation is a visionary artist who contributes to the greater good of humanity.**

♓ **When expressed through a lower frequency of manifestation is a delusional decision to stay in victim/martyrdom situations out of unresolved guilt and shame.**

♓ **Glyph of the two fishes representing the Cosmos swimming forward, backwards, inwards, outwards, etc.**

Anatomy of Pisces: Feet.

Tenants of the twelfth house take on the characteristics of Pisces.

"A way which becomes the way is not the way. A name which becomes the name is not the name."

– Tao Te Ching

Planets in Houses

$\mathcal{H}$12

Pisces ends the cycle of the evolution by the planets. Strong inhabitation of the 12h and Pisces connects us to the Collective Unconscious.

☉ **SUN** We are learning to merge, become clairvoyant, and align with a living spirituality.

☽ **MOON** Emotional acceptance of oneself as a member of a vaster tribe called "humanity".

♀ **VENUS** In her higher octave sign Neptune and the 12th house direct our talents with inspiration to music, dance, the arts, and meditation.

☿ **MERCURY** Is developing a transcendental belief system in alignment with divine order.

♂ **MARS** Empathic and sensitive, the innocence of desire will turn into passion here. Poetry, swimming, the movement of the human form aligned with the Divine delivers growth.

♃ **JUPITER** Here is developing a transcendental belief system of nature. This is a very lucky positive indication of one who embraces Natural Law.

♄ **SATURN** Combined with Neptune is obtaining a realistic awareness of the play of consciousness. This is also called "architecture."

♅ **URANUS** Is the planet known as "Freedom from the Known." We are learning in Pisces to merge, become clairvoyant, and align with a living spirituality.

♆ **NEPTUNE** In the 12th house makes a natural meditator. Self-forgiveness and compassionate understanding for others is the intention of this placement that often comes with considerable talent, inspiration, visionary gifts, musical, and artistic abilities as well. Denial is the distortion of this high frequency and if it is not addressed, suffering is a given.

♇ **PLUTO** In the last sign or house is aligning us with our very deepest soul intention to grow. The innocence of our soul, as a pure co-creator with All That Is, aligns with the frequency of collective humanity and its dreams here. We will have a deep and profound feeling of being connected to Source with this placement.

NB: Pluto and Neptune have been sextile since the 1940s and will be through the 2030s.

This gives us insight into this passage on the larger time frame. Light workers, musicians, and yogis.

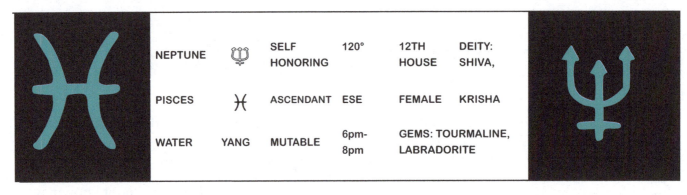

NEPTUNE	♆	SELF HONORING	120°	12TH HOUSE	DEITY: SHIVA,
PISCES	♓	ASCENDANT	ESE	FEMALE	KRISHA
WATER	YANG	MUTABLE	6pm-8pm	GEMS: TOURMALINE, LABRADORITE	

Remember who you were before you came here and you shall never fear again.
—Jamie Hendon

PISCES KEY CONCEPTS

- Returning to Source/God/Goddess.

- Spirituality as a lifestyle.

- Meditation and contemplation of All That Is.

- Dissolve barriers, illusions, and limiting beliefs.

- Face disillusionment to overcome consensus acceptance of the Known.

- Embrace transcendence through unity consciousness.

RIGHT ACTION FOR PISCES

AUTHENTICITY To live a life of talent, mysticism, unconditional, and unlimited love.

INTEGRITY Finding the most aligned and natural way to add spirituality to your life.

OVERCOMING VICTIM MARTYRDOM In your personal life or for the collective, you must find equality and love, living on the two-way street of true loving kindness.

ENRICHING Self and others through overcoming shame and guilt.

DISILLUSIONMENT Confusion, existentialist disorientation, futility, alienation, and escapism lead us to a shift of perspective and finally to a new orientation within the cosmos.

COMPASSION Forgiveness of the self eventually leads us to forgive others and align with the universe in a way that we are uplifted and can also help others.

SPIRITUALITY The path to experience interdependence with All That Is.

The Natural Laws of Pisces ♓12

Neptune is the archetype that signifies our core evolutionary interconnection with the Source of Creation.

We explore the nature of consciousness through experiences of our interdependence.

Study your Neptune by sign, house, and position—in order to evolve.

Pisces is the archetype that leads us to find Spiritual Growth.

Pisces is our spiritual stage of life. Here, we learn to connect our lives to All That Is.

The interdependent evolutionary condition is signified by Neptune.

Wherever we find the sign Pisces or the house in which Neptune resides, we will find our style of meditation and connection to the numinal.

MANTRA
Gobinday Mukunday Udaaray
Apaaray Hariang Kariang
Nirnamay Akamay

Meaning:
- Gobinde   Sustaining
- Mukanday   Liberating
- Udaaray   Enlightening
- Aparray   Infinite
- Hariang   Destroyer
- Kariang,   Creator
- Nirnamay Nameless
- Akamay   Desire-less

This mantra is used to break through deep-seated blocks.
Yogi Bhajan says it is used to "cleanse the subconscious mind," and "it balances the hemispheres of the brain, bringing compassion and patience to the one who meditates on it."

"Find the origination point in the Source of the Cosmos."

–Patricia Albere

NEPTUNE IN THE FIRST HOUSE

Before you embody your spirituality, you might feel disembodied. It is a new beginning because in this life you can learn to vibrate with the Universe in your own way. Your desires are spiritual, and until you can align with your Soul's intentions, you will be disoriented. You will project a type of contrapuntal juxtaposition need onto the world around you as you find your special destiny and learn how to fulfill it on your own terms. Competition is an eye-opener, because Neptune is about sharing, caring, and the soul's journey.

NEPTUNE IN THE SECOND HOUSE

Spirituality and money. Art and survival. Learning to align values and self-worth with a life that has meaning. Discovering the talent and the will to succeed. Eventually, we lean into a life that knows the art of living, through a mix of spiritual values that underly all meaning. Self-worth must derive from compassionate stances and loving kindness. Survival issues and codependency must garner insights into the real interdependency of the Universe.

NEPTUNE IN THE THIRD HOUSE

Neptune delivers the download capacity that the Cosmos provides for us through contemplative lifestyles. Meditation, automatic writing, poetry, lecturing, teaching are all vehicles to invite the multiverse into the depository called "the mind". Eventually, there is a need to transcend the limits of the intellect and use the heart to assist in learning how to communicate with others and the Universe.

NEPTUNE IN THE FOURTH HOUSE

Traumas in the emotional body will be worked through in family scenarios. Spiraling up through meditation, bliss, and deep contemplation can bring enlightening awareness. Spiraling down through codependency and blame can lead to lunacy, ferocity, and madness. The intention for freedom here is to mature the ego. Disillusionment will ensue if expectations are attached to outcome of nurturing or being nurtured.

NEPTUNE IN THE FIFTH HOUSE

Creativity and glamour, a strength of purpose, and a desire to play and celebrate life is often worked out through children or creative self-expression. Tech pioneering and other creative pursuits that require being a few steps ahead of the crowd lead to a leadership position, especially if it serves the greater good. Connecting with community to share the accolades that may derive from creative self-actualization uplifts the karma and furthers evolution. Disillusionment arises from a narcissistic need for recognition.

NEPTUNE IN THE SIXTH HOUSE

Integrating a more subtle experience of living in the soul cage and helping the Earth is the intention of this position. Recapitulation, meditation, Holotropic breathing, kundalini yoga, and other daily practices which are repetitive help Virgo improve. Listening to positive affirmations, enjoying the uplifting frequency of mantras and all other tools to liberate oneself from guilt and shame as well as guilt and anger may also help. Disillusionment results when the ideal of perfection is ridiculous.

Directions

NEPTUNE IN THE SEVENTH HOUSE

The intention here is to learn how to navigate partnerships realistically. Integrating inspiration into a societal context creates a challenge as you find balance between your unique desires to interact and the actual reality of the needs of others. Balance, fairness, sharing, managed expectations, listening without attachment to the outcome, all help to overcome the disillusionments needed to mature.

NEPTUNE IN THE EIGHTH HOUSE

Integrity on how to attract resources, share love with truth and live with basic goodness are lessons of how to merge and co-create. The intrinsic surrender required by 8h tenants must be met with self-empowerment. Disillusionment is a result of an inability to recognize the actual intention of the self and others. This is a result of a faked intimacy and a desire to use the energy or power projected onto others. Lessons about the sacredness of marriage and partnership also lead to evolutionary steps forward.

NEPTUNE IN THE NINTH HOUSE

The need to leave behind outworn beliefs and ways of seeing reality will lead to a perception of Natural Law that is experiential, palpable, and even teachable with this position. Freedom to explore a diversity of ideas, philosophies, religions or other advanced ways of understanding the Cosmos must be attained. The New Age and all evolution through the inter-dependent stage will show some connection between Neptune and Jupiter and the 9h. Disillusionment is a natural experience as compassionate understanding for the reality of the evolutionary condition of everything in the Cosmos is recognized and accepted as it is.

NEPTUNE IN THE TENTH HOUSE

In the Spiritual Stages of evolution, this house always represents the desire to end the old, established hierarchal order and find freedom in a social context. Learning to inspire the Old Guard is par for the course. The path through this is to find your own enlightened position in the society, community, family or scenarios where you have authority or expertise. Maturity comes through disillusionment with outer authority. My mantra for this: "There is no outside."

NEPTUNE IN THE ELEVENTH HOUSE

This house represents the stage of individuality, uniqueness, not being a copy of others, may lead one to a path of recognition for being strange, gifted or just different. Eventually, the reality that this need to be appreciated for a unique stance or position is just a part of the path of evolution that will require humility or severe disillusionment and trauma will ensue. The goal is to make a difference to your community or humanity with your unique gifts.

NEPTUNE IN THE TWELFTH HOUSE

"Ultimate Meaning" is now going to give way to the experience of the numinous. Real spirituality must be lived through meditation, compassion, and any tool that delivers the perception of the interdependence in the Universe. Disillusionment derives from moving through limiting religious or spiritual beliefs.

Pluto Neptune

The sextile ends and Yogi Bhajan and the Mayan Calendar tell us we will have either succeeded in bridging the New Age of Aquarius or humanity will be rebuilding itself around 2036.

From 2043 when Pluto enters Pisces, Neptune and Pluto are out of orb of the sextile as Pluto travels through Pisces. In 2052, Neptune squares Pluto from Gemini.

Neptune and Pluto have been moving in a sextile aspect since the early 1940's.

The sextile is a sixty degree aspect, which is in the Crescent Phase.

Sextiles denote help from the *Uni-verse* and opportunities for growth, development, and self-expression that is helped by Cosmic waves.

The expression of Neptune and Pluto in this helpful aspect points to humanity's work on the bridge to build the Aquarian Age.

The sextile generations are:
- Pluto/Leo-Neptune/ Libra
- Pluto/Virgo Neptune/Scorpio
- Pluto/Libra - Neptune/Sagittarius
- Pluto/Scorpio - Neptune/Capricorn
- Pluto/Sagittarius - Neptune/Aquarius
- Pluto/Capricorn - Neptune/Pisces 2012-2024

CRYSTAL SOULS
Pluto in Pisces

♇♇ 12

9 MARCH 2043 0: 47 UT •D

1 SEPTEMBER 2043 3:31 AM UT •R

19 JANUARY 2044 09: 32 AM UT •D

PLUTO STAYS IN PISCES UNTIL 2067

PLUTO IN THE TWELFTH HOUSE

Assuming that the rest of the chart supports the desire to realize the ultimate meaning for life, Pluto here aligns us to living merged with the Cosmos, Gaia, and our Soul.

This is a result of having looked honestly at emotional co-dependence to the point where we can transcend needing to believe everyone is innocent.

We must also see the play of shadow and light to completely be harmonious with Natural Law.

We must be willing to overcome limiting beliefs as well as spiritual materialism. As the East meets the West, many embrace spirituality like a blanket, instead of as a self-empowering tool.

Instead of ingesting dogma, we must be willing to feel our way through our life.

As we progress, a total ability to know oneself is the result of using these emotional tools, feeling, sensing, observing, caring, tuning in.

Meditation, time spent alone or in nature, and compassion are essential.

The evolutionary mantra for the Pluto in PISCES generation **2043–2067** is:

"I use my connection to the Cosmos to vibrate with its bounty, beauty, bliss and compassion."

If Pluto is in your 12th house or strongly aspecting Neptune, as in the four decade sextile between these two giant Goddess energies, you will need to learn how to overcome guilt, shame, and anger to earn this good frequency. Forgiveness is required. As Bob Dylan would say: "You're gotta serve somebody..."

We learn to love in the 12th house and in Pisces. This is a larger love than personal love, it is tenderhearted compassion and true caring for the well-being of all.

This archetype, in a negative expression, correlates with Victim/Martyrdom. The Cosmos feels like an ocean that can keep you adrift through unconditional love, compassion, kindness to others, and real love for your own eternal self.

The need to learn that you are a part of the Cosmos comes to a level of completion here. It is a stage of merging into the Cosmos, knowing you are an eternal part of Creation itself.

"The most difficult task in living is not to trust in what is seen, but rather to intuit and trust in what is unseen."
—Jenny Boully

Nostradamus

"Events of human origin are uncertain, but all is regulated and governed by the incalculable power of God, inspiring us not through drunken fury nor by frantic movement, but through the influences of the stars."
—**Nostradamus**

Michel de Notredame, is better known as Nostradamus, and he is among the most famous astrologers who ever lived. His work and prophecies are still published, translated, and contemplated 465 years after his writings.

Mercury rules the written word and his Sun is conjunct Mercury, Pallas Athena, and Neptune. Neptune lives outside of time and space. Pallas Athena is a puzzle solver as she sees the interdependence of scenarios, people, places, etc. Neptune is also attributed to our interdependence, thus he was able to see connections that were not yet visible to his collective.

As Magellan's ships arrived in tribal waters in the late 1400s, they were only visible to the Shaman. He actually had to teach his community to believe they were there. Believing is seeing.

Pluto in Sagittarius is another example of a soul deeply merged with All That Is. His Jupiter in Cancer rules his Pluto. The Moon in Scorpio, in the 8h, and Jupiter in Cancer, along with Pluto in the 9h work together. He was able to deeply intuit Natural Law.

The Moon in the 8h may also explain why he lost many of his own friends and family to the plague. His Uranus in Pisces squares Pluto, challenging him to overcome traumas, perhaps through seeing through to non linear time and space reality. His Uranus is also conjunct Vesta, the asteroid correlating to sacred work.

The heavy Capricorn in the MidHeaven shows his leadership abilities and fame. His Chiron at 29 Cancer reveal the urgency of his healing work.

In EA, his Moon in Scorpio in the 8th house—would give him an ability to pierce Natural Law to co-create with the Cosmos. He used his own gift of scrying to tune into the Cosmos.

Neptune also certainly helped him to pierce the veils. He continues to inspire the masses with his ability to learn from the Cosmos. His collective visions are still unfolding. I am sure he is still learning inside and outside of space and time as he continues to Vibrate With the Cosmos.

Natal Chart Pisces ♓ Stellium

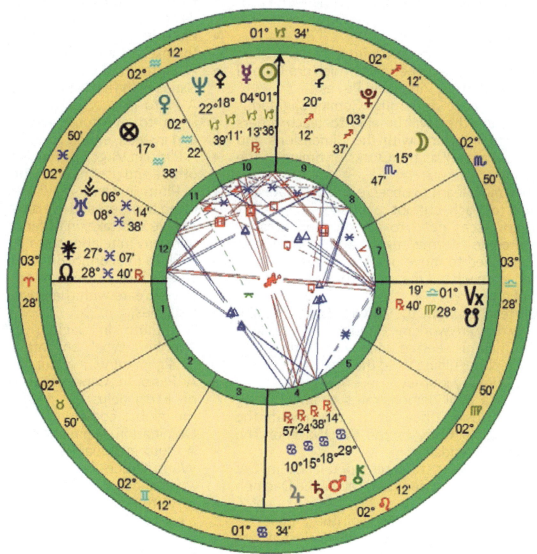

Nostradamus
14 Dec 1555
12:00 pm
Provins, France
source Marc Penfield

Nostradamas
Male Chart
14 Dec 1503 OS, Thu
12:00 pm LMT –0:19:20
st remy, France
46°N46' 004°E50'
Geocentric
Tropical
Porphyry
Mean Node
Rating AA
Astrologer, Prophet

Vᴳx 6°♓	♅ 6°♓	⚶ 27°♓	☊ 28°♓
VERTEX	URANUS	JUNO	NORTH NODE

124

Daemon Soul

Deva is a Sanskrit word meaning "Being of Light," an appropriate name as Deva sing light out of the primordial darkness to create forms for Being.-Jacquelyn E. Lane

- Daemon Soul is a term that originally derives from the work of C. J. Jung. Devas and Devic Beings guide us all. Those of us here on Earth open enough to perceive to these Devas—are called Daemon Souls.
- Daemon Souls are born with a predominance of the mutable archetypes, which are Gemini and Sagittarius, Virgo, and Pisces.
- If they have a strong Gemini/Sagittarius signature, they will be able to teach others how to interface with the dimensions and portals as well as the Clocks or timing of the Cosmos.
- They must learn to observe and correlate and then to teach, but not to preach.
- Virgo/Pisces need to act on their dreams, overcome shame/anger, and shame/fear. They need to move out of analysis/paralysis and learn what it means to enrich themselves and others.
- EA teaches what the Natural Laws are, and how they are working. Evolutionary Astrology can help us see the underlying Natural Law principles, guiding us to the next steps of the evolutionary journey.
- When a soul demonstrates sharing, caring and inclusion they are in touch with the impeccable Unity of the 9th Wave of The Mayan Calendar.
- This correlates to interdependence in EA. These are the actions that reveal the Daemon Soul.
- Those who pose as Spiritual, pose as Evolutionary, yet love and inclusion are not the badge on their sleeve have much work to do in the first stage of Spirituality. The second stage involves teaching and a gentleness is found as that stage progresses.

- Pluto in Aries/1h are pioneers. They are doing something new this time.
- Pluto in Taurus/2h have to learn to survive, using their inherent talents to earn a living.
- Pluto in Gemini/3h are learning to think for themselves and will question authority.
- A Pluto in Cancer/4h person has survival issues with family members.
- A Pluto in Leo/5h individual will eventually learn to overcome narcissistic tendencies, and instead, enrich the community.
- A Pluto in Virgo/6h type will ultimately serve others and use their intuition to stay healthy.
- A Pluto in Libra/7h will eventually learn to listen to others and live on the two-way-street of give and take, in order to find balance and harmony in relationships.
- A Pluto in Scorpio/8h will marry, discovering true intimacy. The most advanced souls learn to co-create with the Cosmos without power struggles.
- A Pluto in Sagittarius/9h is a "Greta Thunberg-type" enlightening us about living in alignment with Natural Law.
- A Pluto in Capricorn/10h soul's presence on Earth helps us all raise the vibration of the global community as we leave behind Domination/Submission scenarios.
- A Pluto in Aquarius/11h is part of the New World Order. They are here to innovate and sever those ways of living that limit our way forward. Trauma, crisis, and change are often a part of the path forward.
- Pluto in Pisces/12h sees the Impeccable Unity. These souls mean business in this life. They intend to dissolve the obstacles which occlude their perception of the interconnectedness of all life. They will work to merge, dissolve, become disillusioned, and align with the transcendental pull that calls them to align to a higher intelligence.

Pluto Paradigm

THE EA STEPS TO SELF EMPOWERMENT
Follow these steps to understand the karmic necessities the soul has to encounter.

PLUTO IN THE 12 SIGNS/HOUSES

Pluto spends between12-20 years in a sign. Each chapter has the dates that Pluto was in one of the 12 signs. The sign and house in which your Pluto resides describes the lessons of your Soul's mission

PLUTO AND MARS
Pluto uses Mars to set up the desires the Soul wishes to explore.

PLUTO AND THE NODES
The basic element of the Pluto Paradigm is the Nodes of the Moon. The South Node is generally inward, downward, backwards motion, and correlates to past lives.

The North Node describe upward, outward and forward motion in this life. It show us our fate and goals. We need to achieve the goals of the Soul through the North Node.

The relationship between the planetary rulers of the South and North Node by house, phase, and aspect delineate where the karmic necessities for evolutionary growth will take place.

Pluto's involvement with the Nodes reveals special information about the goals of the Soul, the direction that must be worked on, as well as those aspects of mundane life that must be experienced for growth to occur.

PLUTO CONJUNCT THE SOUTH NODE

One of the three conditions is present:
- **No blocks: The doors to evolve are wide open because the Soul has such a strong evolutionary pure intention for growth. Gifts from birth, inherent powers to be shared with others.**
- **Blocks: The Soul avoided the need to transform. All intention for ego-based manifestation will be blocked. The Soul needs to release its self-aggrandizement or the tendency to further their own agendas and abuse power.**
- **A mixture of blockage: Reliving the past. Depending on the Soul's ability to change, release, and grow, these three conditions will be imposed.**

PLUTO CONJUNCT THE NORTH NODE
The soul worked on their evolutionary intent so purely, they don't need the polarity point of Pluto. The North Node alone will be so focused on the path forward with the intensity of Pluto conjunct.

ABOUT THE AUTHOR

Tashi Powers, Astrologer to the stars, and an acknowledged Vastu Master has worked as a professional Evolutionary Astrologer (EA) for over three decades. Recognized as one of the Best Global Astrologers, she has clients around the world and is a regular on RAMA TV, with an audience of over 50,000 blessed Kundalini Yoga/Dharma practitioners.

During her career, Tashi has read the charts of acclaimed music artists, The Rolling Stones, The Bee Gees, Madonna, George Harrison, Hollywood stars, Denise Richards, Steven Seagal, Robert Pattinson, and industry moguls including The Marciano Brothers (Guess), and Canadian Rocker, Serena Ryder, as well as many other amazing souls, who she was granted the grace to assist with their evolutionary journey.

She is deeply dedicated to supporting individuals on their spiritual journeys to both successfully meet and excel at their personal evolutionary challenges. Tashi has developed a unique practice and approach which uses Vastu and Evolutionary Astrology to help her clients to use their success responsibly, manage success and/or develop successful strategies.

Her first book, The Mysteries of the Venus Pentagram, deciphers the cycles of Venus.. This is Tashi's second book. She has written this handbook on the basics of Evolutionary Astrology for her students, and to leave a legacy for future astrologers and mystics who wish to co-create with the Cosmos.

The Evolutionary Astrological principles herein that she learned from her mentor, Jeffrey Wolf Green, are the foundation of her own unique lens of how to describe evolutionary growth and Natural Law.

Tao Te Ching - Lao Tzu -Chapter 15

The ancient Masters are profound and subtle.
Embracing a wisdom that is unfathomable.
It is not easy to describe it—we can only emulate their actions.
They are careful—as if crossing an iced-over stream.
Alert as a warrior deep in enemy territory—
Courteous as a gracious guest.
Fluid like melting ice.
Shapable like a block of wood.
Receptive as a green spring valley.
Clear as a container of water.
Do you have the patience to wait until your mud settles and the water is clear?
Can you remain still until the right action arises spontaneously?
The Master doesn't expect fulfillment.
Her non-attachment to outcome
Allows her to be present,
So she can embrace life.

www.enlighteningtimes.com/store

@tashiastrodakini

www.facebook.com/astrodakini

Other Essential Books by Tashi Powers

Tashi's original, practical guide on using directions to attract abundance, health, and wellbeing. Drawing from both Eastern and Western world traditions including Vedic and Evolutionary Astrology, her original approach also includes treasures from feng shui, geomancy, the ley line system, and sacred compass directions.

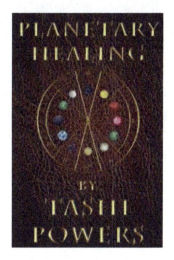

This new book shows how to connect your sun sign and planetary energies with healing gems and stones to create a more fulfilling, healthy life. You will learn step-by-step techniques including planetary mantras and yantras, that are personalized to help you overcome life's challenges and reach your true potential.

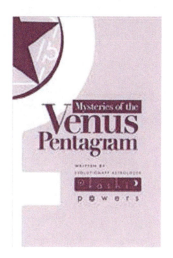

This is Tashi's first and now classic astrology book, which is still available in its original first edition. In its pages, she unveils at long last the Mysteries of the Venus Pentagram. This book will show you how the principles of the Venus cycle operate from her appearance as a Morning Star and also as the brightest Evening Star in our sky. You will learn how the Venus Pentagram Points take form over time and about their impact on world events and how to apply this ancient star wisdom to successfully navigate the Venus energy in your own life.

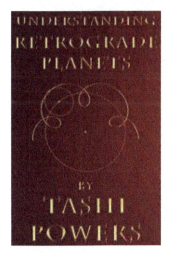

Planetary retrogrades are the Universe's way of providing us with a second chance to review and redo, revise and recreate, and remake yourself and others. Tashi's new book addresses not only Mercury, but all the planets and the unique opportunities presented when they are in retrograde motion.

This is the classic book on applying the mysteries of Venus, now reissued in a practical workbook format and updated through 2023. Based on both modern technology and sacred geometry, Tashi's pentagram mandala system offers a holistic approach to discover the relationships, resources, and values that will illuminate the path of higher love and prosperity.

26059612R00079